CEN

D0539273

tal
Shorthair Cat

◇

By Maria Graciete Coelho

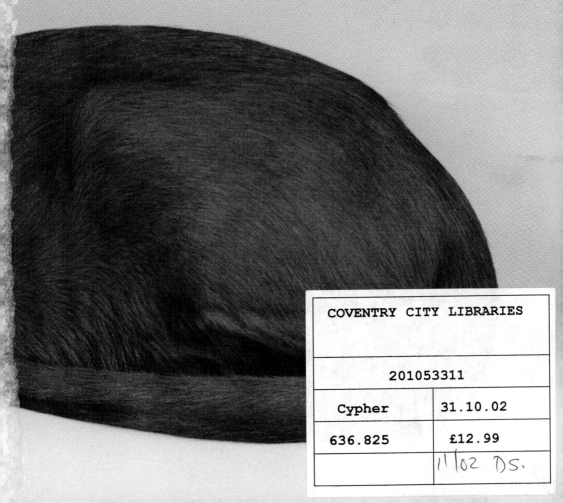

COVENTRY CITY LIBRARIES	
201053311	
Cypher	31.10.02
636.825	£12.99
	11/02 DS.

Contents

PUBLISHED IN THE UNITED KINGDOM BY:

INTERPET
PUBLISHING

Vincent Lane, Dorking   Surrey RH4 3YX   England

ISBN 1-84286-040-2

All rights reserved.
No part of this book may be reproduced in any form, by photostat, scanner, microfilm,
xerography or any other means, or incorporated into any information retrieval system,
electronic or mechanical, without the written permission of the copyright owner.

Copyright © 2001 Animalia Books, S.L.   Cover patent pending. Printed in Korea.

PHOTO CREDITS:
Photographs by Isabelle Francais, Cheryl Ertelt, Alan Robinson, Erin Winters,
with additional photographs by The Animal Health Trust of England,
M W Brim, Cat Fanciers Association, Carolina Biological Supply,
Fleabusters Rx for Fleas, J R Hayden, RBP, Interpet, Dwight R Kuhn,
Dr Dennis Kunkel, Phototake, Jean Claude Revy and W B Saunders Company.

If the Persian, in its build, is the Bulldog of the cat fancy, then the Siamese is the Greyhound. These breeds represent the extremes of anatomical deviation from the typical form of domestic cats, of which the moggie, or mongrel, is the ancestral archetype. They are the 'designer' breeds that are forever pushing the limits of visual expression. With such felines, cat owners rarely take a middle-ground viewpoint—they either love them or hate them.

The Persian and the Siamese are two of the three great breed` pillars around which all other breeds have been developed—the third is the British Shorthair and its close relatives. The Oriental Shorthair derived from

the Siamese. It is, roughly speaking, a Siamese of another colour. In the USA, the Oriental Shorthair is the name given to cats of Siamese conformation exhibiting colours not accepted within the breed standards of the Siamese. In the UK and Continental Europe, the self-coloured Siamese are termed Foreigns and just the tabbies, torties and spotted tabbies of Siamese conformation are called Orientals. The history of the Oriental Shorthair began in the 1950s when Siamese breeders began experimental programmes in an attempt to recreate a solid colour known to have existed in the Siamese during the 19th century. The mutations created by these experiments (which

The Oriental Shorthair derived from the Siamese and might be considered a Siamese of a different colour.

The Oriental Shorthair came into being when Siamese breeders tried to recreate a solid-coloured cat.

eventually led to the Havana Brown) became the Oriental Shorthair.

EARLY SIAMESE COLOURS

In the earliest years of the hobby, there were a number of Siamese that had a much darker body colour than was typical for the breed. There were others that had a solid dark brown colour. The solid-coloured individuals were called self-chocolate Siamese. Interestingly, a brown cat was exhibited in Britain during 1894 under the name of Swiss Mountain Cat.

In that same year, two cats with the names of Master Timkey Brown and Granny Grumps were exhibited. They were described as being burnished chestnut with a greenish-blue eye colour. Two other solid, or self, colours present in those days were the black and the blue. There were also blue-pointed and chocolate-pointed individuals.

The situation became the source of growing controversy. Eventually, in the 1920s, the vexed question of what constituted a Siamese was finally addressed. The Siamese Cat Club of Britain decreed that only blue-eyed cats displaying the pointed coat pattern would be eligible for competition. All others were regarded as being unwanted Siamese variants. The self-colours—black, blue and chocolate—disappeared from the hobby. The blue- and chocolate-pointed colours became less widely seen, as they were regarded as being of poor colour. The darker bodied forms vanished from the hobby because they had yellow- to amber-coloured eyes. Somewhat later, in 1936, the blue-pointed variety was given official recognition. The chocolate-pointed followed in 1949.

THE *CAT BOOK OF POEMS*

What was not known at that time was that each of the other colour types was actually every bit as deserving of the name Siamese as was the breed that became known under that name. The brown cat of Siam, along with 22 other varieties, was known to have existed in Siam (now called Thailand) for many centuries.

The popular breed known as the Burmese may have derived from dark-bodied or self-coloured cats that differed in body type from the Siamese.

These colour varieties are documented and illustrated in a treatise called the *Tamra Maew.* This now famous script is known as the *Cat Book of Poems,* written circa 1350–1757. One of the cats in that work was called the *Thong Daeng*, meaning 'copper.' Another cat was called the *Wichien Maas*, meaning 'Moon Diamond.' It was the Moon Diamond that was exhibited at the 1871 show under the name of Siamese.

The all-blue cat was known as Si-Sawat or Dork Lao, meaning 'Lao flower.' It is known today in the Western world as the Korat breed. The all-black cats were known under various names, such as Goanjar, Grajorg and Hin Thoat. There was even an albino called Tupolapate.

THE COPPER CAT

It is not known whether the Thong Daeng was a self-coloured cat or a very dark-bodied pointed breed. The general consensus of opinion is that it was a self-colour. If this is so, we must assume that breeders in those past centuries did not distinguish between it and the dark-bodied forms.

In 1930 the dark-body type was introduced from Burma (now Myanmar) to the cat fancy in America. Its genetic base was

THE CRYSTAL PALACE SHOW

On 13 July 1871, an event took place that changed the world of the domestic cat. In the Crystal Palace at Sydenham, London, the world's first all-breed cat show took place. It was organised by Harrison Weir (1824–1906), a noted animal artist and great lover of British Shorthairs.

The success of the cat show saw Weir become a noted cat judge and author. Today he is regarded as the 'father of the cat fancy.' In his later years he complained that Eastern cats were causing the demise of his beloved British Shorthairs. This did not endear him to Persian owners, whose cats were now beginning to dominate the hobby.

The Crystal Palace show attracted thousands of people, many of whom had never seen, or were not even aware of, some of the breed types. On display were many British Shorthairs, Siamese, Manx and a wild cat. Also present was a cat reputed to be direct from Persia. It was said to have a delightful person-ality and its colour was black, grey and white. White Persians were also on view. For many visitors these were by far the most impressive exhibits, with their pale blue eyes and flowing fur.

The Tonkinese developed from Burmese-Siamese matings.

The Korat is one of the non-pointed Siamese-type breeds. .

The Havana received its name because its coat is supposed to be the colour of a Havana cigar. Unfortunately, Havana cigars are found in all shades of brown, none of which is the colour of the Havana cat.

established to be in the same series as the Siamese but was created by a totally separate mutation. It was developed to become the highly popular Burmese. It is probable that the dark versions of the Siamese appearing in the early cat shows were, in fact, Burmese or hybrids of Burmese and Siamese. Such hybrids create the breed known as the Tonkinese.

SIAMESE GENE POOL

Bringing together all of the information we now have on the cats of Thailand, feline genetics and the development of the Siamese, it is clear that the breed had a mixed genotype pool by the late 19th century. The genes for colour restriction—meaning Siamese and Burmese, together with the dilution gene that creates blue and lilac—were present. So too was the recessive gene that created the self-brown

(chocolate) and the dominant gene that resulted in black.

The potential to split this genotype back into its historical state began the moment the Siamese Cat Club redefined the Siamese. Today that division is complete. There now exist in the cat fancy breeds that represent the original genotypes of the *Tamra Maew*. These breeds are the Siamese, Burmese, Korat and Oriental Shorthair in its numerous colour forms.

HAVANA BROWN

In 1951, leading British breeders crossed domestic shorthairs and Russian Blues with seal-point Siamese in the hope of obtaining a self-chocolate cat of Siamese type. The most notable of these breeders, together with their cattery names, were Armitage Hargreaves (Laurentide), Elsie Fischer (Praha) and Baronesss von Ullmann (Roofspringer).

However, before any of these breeders were able to produce a self-chocolate, another breeder, Mrs Monro-Smith, did just that by accident in 1952. She was trying to create a true black-pointed Siamese by crossing a seal-point with a black shorthaired Siamese hybrid. She failed in that endeavour, but in the litter was a most handsome brown male of Siamese type.

She named it Elmtower Bronze Idol.

A year later, Elsie Fischer paired a seal-point Siamese with one of her black shorthaired Siamese hybrids. The result was the self-chocolate Praha Gypka. The other breeders also succeeded in producing self-chocolates, in the case of Armitage Hargreaves via the Russian Blue route. It was decided to name the breed Havana after the cigar of that colour. It has also been suggested that it was named after the Havana Brown rabbit breed.

At this point in the text, an important comment needs to be made. Most books and accounts of the development of the Havana state that seal-point Siamese were used in the various matings. This can be misleading. If these cats were seal-points, then genetically they could not have been pure-breeding (homozygous) for seal. They must have been carrying

The Russian Blue was used extensively to produce a self-chocolate Siamese-type cat.

THE HAVANA BROWN

A self-brown Siamese was developed in England. It could not be called a Siamese as it was a self colour. It was therefore called Havana. However, because the GCCF would not accept the name Havana, it was called the Chestnut Foreign Shorthair and placed into the Foreign Section of breeds in the GCCF classification. A few years later, the name Havana was accepted and the breed remained in the Foreign Shorthair group. The Havana was exported to the USA, where it was called Havana Brown.

The Havana Brown of America developed onwards as a quite separate breed to that in Britain—it was not crossed back to the Siamese and lost certain of its Siamese type. When the British Foreign Shorthairs of Siamese type were exported to America, it was decided to call them Oriental Shorthairs. Clearly, the name Havana for the Oriental Shorthair self-brown would create confusion with the now separate breed of that name—the Havana Brown. So, the Americans gave the brown the name of Chestnut. Subsequently, the British also used the term Oriental Shorthair for the group of cats that are Siamese, but in a non-Siamese patterned form. The name Havana was retained for the self-brown variety. Thus, the Chestnut Oriental Shorthair of America is the same as the Havana Oriental Shorthair of Britain and elsewhere.

in hidden form (genetically called 'spilt for') the gene for chocolate.

Alternatively, they were not seal-point but chocolate-point, thus being homozygous for this colour. Visually, a genetically dark chocolate might look like a seal-point. It might have been registered as such, especially during the 1950s when the chocolate-point was not commonly seen.

NEW COLOUR BREEDS

Given that the dilution gene was present in the Havana, it was not long before the self-lilac was produced and called the Foreign Lilac. The same gene working on the seal colour (which is genetically black) produced the Foreign Blue. The Foreign Black and the Foreign White also became established, and interest in the non-pointed Siamese gained momentum.

THE ORIENTAL SPOTTED TABBY
During the 1960s, at about the same time the Foreign White was being developed, Angela Sayer, a noted English breeder, was involved in creating a Siamese-bodied tabby. In the process, a cat was produced with broken tabby markings not unlike the cats seen in ancient Egyptian paintings. She commenced a second programme for cats she called Mau (meaning 'cat' in Egyptian), using Siamese and the Foreign Havana.

GENETICS OF THE HAVANA

Readers may wonder why Siamese breeders crossed their cats to either a domestic black cat, such as the British Shorthair, or to the Russian Blue, in an effort to obtain a self-chocolate. The reason was to try to separate the paired genes controlling the Siamese pattern cs from that which created the self-chocolate b. In both instances the genes involved are called recessive. This means they must be present in both parents, each having the genotype cscsbb, before they are manifested in the parent, thus in their offspring.

If the Siamese is paired to a non-Siamese, then none of the offspring can inherit these genes from both parents. They will display neither the Siamese pattern nor the chocolate colour. However, all the offspring will carry one gene for the pattern and the colour—both inherited from the Siamese. The litter, presupposing there are no other compatible recessive genes in either parent, will comprise black kittens.

These offspring, each carrying a gene for both Siamese and chocolate, if mated will create the potential for the single genes to become pairs again in their offspring. However, they will not necessarily become two pairs in the same individual. The Siamese pattern and the self-colour have thus been separated.

The theoretical ratio of colour expectations from this mating is nine black, three seal-point Siamese, three self-chocolate (Havana) and one chocolate-point Siamese. There is thus an 18.75% chance of obtaining the Havana.

When the Russian Blue crossing was used, this made the genotype expectations more complicated because it introduced the gene for dilution. This will result in the potential for the self-blue as well as the self-lilac to appear in litters. In the early days of the Havana, any blues produced were in fact registered as Russian Blues. It was not ever necessary to use the Russian Blue, but its choice was deliberate. It was hoped the Russian Blue conformation would benefit from matings to the Siamese.

The Egyptian Mau was created by crossing the Siamese and the Foreign Havana.

The Havana Brown, as the breed is known in America, is a self-brown Siamese.

However, a similar programme in America, via a different route, had been in hand for a longer period to create the breed now called the Egyptian Mau. The Sayer Mau name was dropped and replaced by Oriental Spotted Tabby. It was decided by the Governing Council of the Cat Fancy (GCCF) in Britain that all non-self cats of Siamese type would be called Oriental, with all the self-colours being called Foreign.

MORE COLOURS, PATTERNS & CONFUSION

With the passage of more years, the number of other colours and patterns increased. Eventually, problems began to emerge over the way the non-pointed Siamese were classified. The situation was that in the Foreign Section were three blues: Russian, Korat and Foreign Blue (which was the Siamese-based self-blue). There were two whites: the green-eyed Russian White and the blue-eyed Foreign White. There was also the Russian Black and the Foreign Black.

Things were getting very complicated, especially for novices and pet owners. To simplify matters, the Foreign self-coloured Siamese were transferred from the Foreign Section into the more appropriate Oriental Section. However, it was decided they would retain their 'Foreign' nametag.

This did not overcome the problem, because Foreign colours could appear in litters of cats named Oriental Tabby or Oriental Tortoiseshell and so on. It was therefore decided to call all the Foreign self-colours

Oriental selfs, thus Oriental Lilac, Oriental Red, and so on.

It was also decided that the Havana would retain its name on historical grounds, but would be called the Oriental Havana. The Foreign White would become the Oriental Foreign White. These changes did not go down well with breeders.

Six months later it was decided the Havana would be retained in the Oriental Section but that it would simply be called Havana. The Foreign White would likewise retain its name but would also remain in the Oriental Section. This decision was made in 1991 and remains the way that the Oriental Section is classified to this day.

THE BREED IN AMERICA

The Havana was first exported from England to America in 1956, where it was named Havana Brown. It gained recognition by 1959. However, the breed did not then develop as in England by continued crossings to the Siamese. As a consequence, the Havana Brown became a breed unto itself and not aligned to the Siamese.

By 1972 the Foreign Shorthairs of Britain were creating much interest in America. In that year Siamese breeders Peter and Vickie Markstein campaigned to have them all accepted under the name of Oriental Shorthair with no division into 'Foreign.' This happened and they were exhibited in Cat Fanciers

The Oriental Shorthair, whether self-coloured or patterned, is an elegant feline, whose confusing history and development should not discourage cat lovers from acquiring one of these beauties.

The Javanese, as the Oriental Longhair is called in mainland Europe and America, is called Angora by the GCCF, not to be confused with the Turkish Angora breed. The breed was believed to resemble the more ancient Angora cat noted in the history of many longhaired cats.

Federation (CFF) shows during 1976. Thereafter, one association after the other gave them recognition.

However, as the Havana Brown had developed as a separate breed in America, the name 'Havana' could not be applied in that country to the Brown Oriental Shorthair as was done in Britain. It was decided to name the colour Chestnut. The Oriental Shorthair White of America differs with its British counterpart in that both green- and odd-eyed whites are allowed, along with the blue-eyed. Only blue eyes are acceptable in the Foreign White of Britain.

ORIENTAL LONGHAIR
The Oriental Longhair as a breed name is not universally used. In Britain the Cat Association calls this breed the Javanese, as do most European and American feline registries. The GCCF gave longhaired Oriental Shorthairs breed recognition under the name of Angora, an unfortunate choice. Some European clubs call the breed the Mandarin.

The Cat Fanciers Association (CFA) and The International Cat Association (TICA) of America actually call the breed what it is: Oriental Longhair. Its history in Britain traces back to the late 1960s. A planned mating between a Siamese and an Abyssinian resulted in the cinnamon gene being transferred to the hybrid offspring. When these were paired to each other, a cinnamon kitten was produced.

In the process the longhair gene carried by some Abyssinians was also transferred to the hybrids.

This eventually resulted in the longhaired Oriental. The Balinese (longhaired Siamese) was also involved in the subsequent development of the longhair. It was decided to call the new breed Angora, as it resembled the Angora present in the earliest years of the cat fancy. That breed vanished, but was imported back into the Western world from Turkey during 1960s. It reached Europe by the 1970s. As a consequence it was called the Turkish Angora to distinguish it from the British manufactured look-alike.

Unfortunately, the Oriental Longhair has not enjoyed any sort of popularity in Britain even though it has been established for about 30 years. One of the major problems for the breed is that there are problems in producing it. Numerous kittens that cannot be shown as Oriental Longhairs are produced in its litters. They either carry the pointed pattern (thus are Balinese in appearance) or they are Oriental Shorthairs. In spite of the problems, the Oriental Longhair is a breed of undoubted merit. It enables self-colours and full-body patterns to be available to fanciers that are not available in any other longhaired Siamese-based breed.

The Oriental Longhair is prized for offering the only self-coloured and full-body patterns in a longhaired Siamese-type breed.

While graceful and sleek, the Oriental Shorthair is surprisingly hefty and muscular. The breed can be enjoyed in well over 300 different colour combinations.

A Portrait of the

ORIENTAL SHORTHAIR CAT

With it sleek body and angular head, the Oriental Shorthair looks very much an avant-garde feline designed to move with speed in a graceful manner. In its longhaired form, its lines appear softer and less extreme. This gives the potential owner an appealing alternative choice. If you like the look of this breed, you will really be spoilt for choice when it comes to colour and pattern combinations. There are well over 300 to choose from, though not all of these have recognition in Britain and some other countries at this time.

When an Oriental is lifted, most would-be owners are surprised to find it is quite heavy. Its very svelte design totally masks the strong and heavy underlying musculature. This endows it with a hardiness that is not initially apparent from its physical appearance.

BREED STANDARD
The definitive written description of any cat breed is its official standard of points drafted by its national breed club. This is adopted by a national feline registry and is the basis for assessing the breed in any exhibitions run under the rules of that registry. A standard contains many words that are relative states, such as long, short, in proportion to, well-balanced and slender. In the absence of a visual image against which these words can be compared, the standard is actually a rather vague document.

The visual meaning of the standard can only be determined by seeing individuals of the breed adjudged to be good examples. By so doing, the onlooker can gain a more sound understanding of what the standard requires. Each feline registry has it own standard. While this is very similar to all others, it will differ in its wording and in the points that are allotted to the various body parts of the breed.

Potential breeders and exhibitors should obtain the standard appropriate to the association with which their cats are registered. The description here is not that of any single association but has been compiled by reference to numerous of these. It should meet the needs of most owners. Where appropriate, additional comments are given in order to explain certain technical terms.

DESCRIPTION OF THE ORIENTAL SHORTHAIR CAT

Head: Of medium size, the head is long and composed of straight lines that form a triangle when viewed from the front. The lines should commence at the muzzle and continue to the ears, whose outer edges should maintain the lines of the triangle. There should be no whisker pad pinch or break. Allowance should be made for jowls in mature stud males.

When viewed in profile, the shape is again a wedge. There should be a straight line from the top of the head to the tip of the nose. However, some standards allow the straight lines of the head and nose to be separated by a slight change of angle just above the eyes. The nose must be straight with no dip at its tip.

The distance between the eyes should not be less than the width of one eye. A level bite is required, which in turn will favour the correct chin shape. A level bite is where the upper incisor teeth just touch those of the lower jaw. They should not protrude over those of the lower jaw (overshot), nor should the reverse be true (undershot). The head should be supported on a long and slender neck.

Eyes: Oriental in shape, meaning slanted towards the nose. The eyes must be neither protruding nor sunken. They should be free of a squint. This is when the eyes appear to be looking at the nose (cross-eyed). This was a common fault in the Siamese years ago but has now largely been eradicated.

Eye Colour: With the exception of the Foreign White, eye colour in all varieties should be green. In the Foreign White, it should be blue. In the Angora, it should be green in all colours except for the blue- or odd-eyed whites, meaning one eye green, the other blue.

Ears: These should be large—strikingly so when compared to most non-Siamese-based breeds. The ear tips should be pointed and the ear base wide.

Body: This is of medium size, muscular, long and svelte. The abdomen should be tight, meaning not displaying superfluous flesh. The body is tubular and should not be wider at the hips than at the shoulders.

Legs: Slim, fine-boned, but muscular and long. The hind legs should be taller than those of the front.

Paws: Small and oval. There should be five toes on the front feet and four on the rear.

Tail: Thin, long and tapering to a pointed, rather than a blunted, end.

This chocolate tabby Oriental Shorthair exhibits the desirable long and triangular head of the breed.

The body is medium sized, long and svelte, as modestly shown by this Apricot Oriental Shorthair.

It must be free of any sign of bone abnormality. This refers essentially to a kink in the tail. This was common in early Siamese lines but has largely been eradicated by selective breeding.

Coat: Displaying a glossy sheen, the coat is very short, of fine texture and close-lying, meaning lying flat to the body. There is no woolly undercoat. In the Oriental Longhair, the coat is as that of the Shorthair but of a longer length. It is longest on the tail, where it forms a plume. It may also create a small frill around the face and neck and on the underparts. The longest hairs may form gentle waves.

Breed Faults: Faults in any breed are of three basic types. There are anatomical faults applicable to all breeds, those that are breed-specific and those that apply to particular colours and patterns. It is not possible to list all these in this chapter. A small selection of some that might be appropriate to the Oriental Shorthair is given here.

Anatomical faults include matters such as entropion (ingrown eyelashes), bone abnormalities (depressions or protrusions), undershot and overshot jaws, kink of the spine or tail, abnormal number of toes and lack of both testicles descended in the scrotum of males. Breed-specific faults include weak chin, coarse coat texture and some of the general faults applied to all breeds.

Colour and pattern faults would include incorrect eye colour, white hairs or patches anywhere in the coat other than in areas stipulated in the colour or pattern standard, colour not the same down to the roots (unless of a pattern that allows this) and incorrect pattern.

COLOURS & PATTERNS

With over 300 colour and pattern combinations to choose from, it will be appreciated that every one of these cannot be listed here. Some are very popular; others range from less so to extremely rare. The high number of options is created in the following manner.

There are ten solid or self colours, plus white. There are then a number of patterns, each of which can be combined with each of the colours. Certain patterns may also be combined to create more complex combinations, which can in turn be combined with the colours. Additionally, both colours and patterns can be combined with white.

At any one time there are always new colours and/or patterns being developed. Further-more, existing patterns in other breeds, but which are not yet seen in the Oriental, will no doubt

ORIENTAL SHORTHAIR SOLID COLOURS

WHITE Pure white. Occasionally, a few coloured hairs are present in the coat of a kitten. These should disappear by adulthood in all but badly coloured individuals.

BLACK This is called ebony by some registries. It should be jet or coal black. Any rusty tinges in kittens should disappear by adulthood.

BLUE A light or medium blue is preferred. A better description of blue in cats would be slate grey. Genetically, blue is created by a dilution of black.

HAVANA This is a rich chestnut brown. It is the colour that originally instigated what is now the Oriental breed. Havana equates the chocolate of the Siamese. It is called Chestnut in the Oriental Shorthair of some registries, including that of the CFA. It should be noted that the Havana Brown of America is a separate breed to the Oriental Shorthair Havana colour variety.

LILAC This is a grey colour displaying a pinkish hue that gives the coat the impression of a lilac colour. In America it is known as lavender. It is the genetic dilution of Havana.

RED A deep, rich red. In pure-bred cats this is a much more brilliant colour than that seen in the average moggie, which is a more ginger colour. Faint tabby markings may be evident, especially in kittens.

CREAM Described as a cool-toned cream or buff cream, the actual shade will be determined by the shade of red from which it has been created. Genetically, it is the dilution of red. Faint tabby markings may be displayed, especially in kittens.

APRICOT A hot cream with a soft metallic sheen. Faint tabby markings may be evident, especially in kittens. This is one of the latest colours to gain recognition. It is created by a mutation that modifies the effect of the dilution gene on red.

CINNAMON This can be described as a warm cinnamon brown or a light reddish brown. Genetically, it is a lighter version of the Havana created by a different mutation at the same gene locus.

CARAMEL A bluish fawn. The colour is genetically a dilution of cinnamon, but one in which the dilution gene itself is modified by a mutation.

FAWN A warm rosy mushroom, the pinker the better. In the CFA of America, fawn is described as light lavender (lilac of Britain) with pale cocoa overtones. Fawn is the dilution of cinnamon.

appear in the breed during the coming years. In future years, the present bewildering number of varieties may seem quite modest.

In the following description, the colour of the nose leather, paw pads and eye rims are not given in order to save space and repetition. Generally, these colours will correspond to the body colour. In Whites, this will translate to pink.

SOLID COLOURS

The solid colours are white, black, blue, Havana (brown), lilac, red, cream, apricot, cinnamon, caramel and fawn. In each of the solid colours, it is required these be of the same colour down to the hair roots. It is also preferred that there should be no shading, meaning areas of the coat that display a darker/lighter shade than that on the rest of the coat.

In cats, the names applied to colours can appear confusing to the beginner. Different registries may apply different names to the same colour. What is black to one is ebony to another. The most complex colour is brown, which is given many names in cats depending on its shade.

Even experienced breeders can find it difficult to visually distinguish between a shade of a colour and a colour that is actually genetically different. For example, a light shade of Havana may be just that, or it may be a dark shade of cinnamon, which is

INTELLECTUAL EXPRESSION

With so much energy to burn, the Oriental can get very excited when playing and loves to play games. This may, on occasion, result in over-exuberance, which must be allowed for. Being so athletic, the Oriental is able to effect the actions that will satisfy its curiosity about things.

Whereas heavier built cats may think about investigating a high shelf, they will often lose interest because they know they cannot reach them. Not so for the Oriental. It will reach any shelf. Because it is so 'hyper,' the Oriental always wants to explore.

created by a different gene mutation.

Presently, blue ranges from light to dark. These shades have always been regarded as variations of the same gene mutation. However, the identification of a mutation that modifies

The classic brown tabby pattern has black markings over a brown ground colour.

the action of the dilution gene that creates blue means that, in due course, certain of the blue shades may be given their own specific colour name.

This has happened with the cream, to create the apricot, and with the fawn, to create the caramel. As a final comment, it should be stated that in the Oriental Shorthair self (solid) colours of the GCCF, dark brown is called Havana. However, in the patterned varieties, as well as in the longhaired variety, it is called chocolate.

COAT PATTERNS

Presently, there are nine coat patterns you can choose from. For our purposes, these can be divided into five broad groups: tabby (four varieties), tipped (two varieties), tortoiseshell, bi-colour and composite. Cat registries use their own system to define colour and pattern groups.

Tabby Group: The basic tabby pattern is well known to all cat lovers. The pattern is that of the wild cat (*Felis sylvestris*) from which the domestic cat was developed. Genetically, the name for the tabby is agouti. It has four distinct forms: mackerel, classic (blotched), spotted and ticked.

All colours and patterns in domestic cats have been created by numerous mutations that have altered the agouti pattern and its

colours. The main difference between the various tabbies is with respect to their body markings. The head markings comprise the letter 'M' on the forehead, from which narrow lines pass over the skull.

Mascara lines extend from the eyes to the cheeks. The neck contains unbroken necklaces, while the legs are barred with dark rings. The tail is ringed and its tip should be the solid colour of the other markings.

The tabby is available in all Oriental solid colours as well as silver versions of these. Silver is a sparkling version of the normal pale ground colour. In tabbies, the black-marked pattern is called brown, which is the colour of the ground on which the black pattern is overlaid. However, in the silver tabbies, the pattern is called black.

Tipped Group: The basis of this group is that the hairs are tipped with colour, while the hair root is as near white as possible or a pale shade of the tipped colour, depending on the variety in question. In longhaired cats, there are three grades of tipping, but in shorthairs only two of these are seen due to the shorter hair length. Tipped cats may exhibit any colour accepted in the Oriental Shorthair.

In the smoke pattern, one-third to two-thirds of the hair is

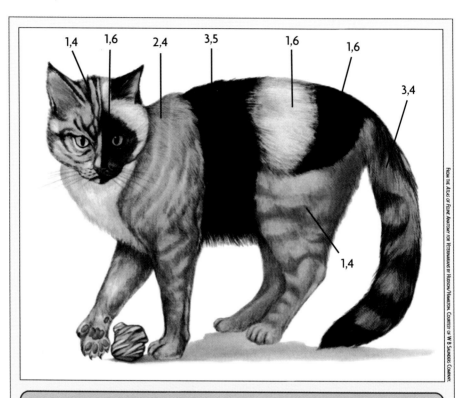

From the Atlas of Feline Anatomy for Veterinarians by Hudson/Hamilton. Courtesy of W B Saunders Company.

PARTICOLOURED CAT

Not a new breed of feline, this 'particoloured cat' illustrates the many possibilities of the feline coat. Since cats come in three basic hair lengths, short, long and rex (curly), all three coat lengths are illustrated here. Additionally, different coat patterns, such as mackerel tabby, Abyssinian and self-coloured, are depicted to demonstrate the differences.

1–3 COAT TYPES
1 Shorthair coat
2 Rex (curly) coat
3 Longhair coat

4–6 COAT COLOUR PATTERNS
4 Mackerel (tabby)
5 Abyssinian
6 Self-coloured

SKIN AND HAIRCOAT OF CATS

Schematic illustration of histologic layers of the integument skin.

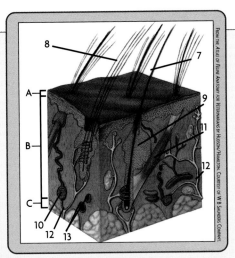

A Epidermis
B Dermis
C Subcutis

7 Primary hair
8 Secondary hairs
9 Area of sebaceous gland
10 Apocrine sweat gland
11 M arrector pili
12 Nerve fibre
13 Cutaneous vessels
14 Tactile hair
15 Fibrous capsule
16 Venous sinus
17 Sensory nerve fibres
18 External root sheath
19 Hair papilla

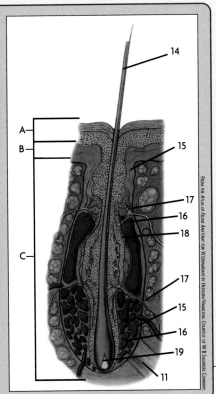

Schematic illustration of a tactile hair (whisker).

From the Atlas of Feline Anatomy for Veterinarians by Hudson/Hamilton. Courtesy of W B Saunders Company.

The bi-colour pattern in Oriental Shorthairs is not recognised by the GCCF, but it is accepted by the American registries.

pigmented over a base as nearly white as possible. In repose, the cat looks like a solid colour. When it moves, the white undercoat is evident, creating a constant colour/white contrast.

In the shaded pattern, the tipping may vary from extending to no more than half the hair length to that which is restricted to the hair tips. The effect is to create darker and lighter areas on the coat. The tabby pattern, in any of its forms, may be superficially apparent. Shading should follow the underlying tabby pattern, so will be darker on the back and sides.

Tortoiseshell: This unusual pattern, also called tortie, is sex-linked and normally restricted to females. Males are possible, but as they are genetic abnormalities, they are invariably sterile. The pattern comprises the base colour, such as black, blue and so on. This is randomly patched and/or mingled with shades of red, cream or beige, depending on the base colour.

The patched hairs may display tabby markings. The head, body, legs and tail should all display some break in the base colour. The head may or may not carry a blaze. The colours black, chocolate and cinnamon are patched with shades of dark and/or light red. The colours blue, lilac, caramel and fawn are patched with shades of cream.

Bi-Colour Group: This colour pattern is not as yet recognised by the GCCF, but is by the major American registries. Any of the colours and patterns accepted in the Oriental can be combined with white to create a bi-colour. The placement and amount of white in this pattern within other breeds vary between British and American associations. Generally, it is preferred that white is present, as a minimum, on the face, feet, legs, chest and underbelly. It is invariably found on the body as well. The tortoise-shell and white of America is called calico.

Composite Patterns: When two or more patterns are combined, they create a complex or composite pattern. At this time the tortie-tabby, also called the torbie, is the only example of this in the Oriental Shorthair of Britain. In this pattern, the tabby is overlaid with patches of red and/or cream.

This usually female-only pattern is sometimes called tortie and is one of the most unusual patterns in the Oriental Shorthair.

Showing off two of the many lovely colours in the breed: (above) The caramel tortie silver-shaded and (below) the cream spotted tabby.

THE PURCHASING PROCESS

Never rush into the purchase of a companion that is to be given the freedom of your home and will become an integral part of your life. A pure-bred cat may live 20 or more years. This is a long time. It is very prudent to take all those steps that will minimise the chances of your ever regretting the choice you make. Once you have decided on the sex, age, reason for purchase (pet, show or breeding) and desired colour pattern, proceed cautiously, heeding all the advice given here. By following a planned process of selection, you will also gain much useful information.

Before the decision to purchase an Oriental Shorthair is made, careful consideration should be given to the implications and responsibilities of cat ownership. If more owners would do this, there would be far fewer half-starved pets roaming our streets or having to live in local animal rescue centres.

OWNER RESPONSIBILITY

The initial cost of an Oriental Shorthair represents only a fraction of its lifetime's cost. The first question is, 'Can you afford one?' The kitten needs vaccinations to protect it against various diseases. Boosters are then required every year. Cat food is more costly than that for dogs. There is also the cost of cat litter every week. Periodic vet checks and treatment for illness or accidents must be allowed for. When holidays are taken, you may need to board the pet at a cattery.

From the outset there will be additional costs apart from that of the kitten. It will need a basket, carrying box, feeding and

DOCUMENTATION

When you take delivery of your kitten, certain paperwork should come with it:

1. Three- to five-generation pedigree.
2. Breeder-signed registration application form or change of owner registration form. This assumes the breeder has registered stock. If they have not, the kitten cannot be registered at a later date. It is worth less than the kitten with registration paperwork. You are not recommended to purchase a kitten from unregistered parents.
3. Certificates of health, vaccination and neutering, if this has been effected. Ideally, it is desirable that the kitten's parents have been tested negative for major diseases. Additionally, the breeder should know the blood group of your kitten. This may be of importance at a later date.
4. Details of worming or other treatments attended.
5. Diet sheet, feeding timetable and brand names of food items used. This diet should be maintained for at least ten days while the kitten adjusts to the trauma of moving home.
6. Signed receipt for monies paid.
7. Signed copy of any guarantees. Not all breeders give a guarantee on the reasonable grounds that once the kitten leaves their care, its onward well-being is no longer under their control.

grooming utensils, scratching post and maybe a collar and a few toys. If you have any doubts at all about being able to supply all these needs, it is best not to obtain a cat.

Other matters also need careful thought. If you are planning to have a family, will your love for the Oriental Shorthair be compromised once a baby arrives? Cats are generally not a problem with family newcomers, providing they are not ignored or treated as being a threat to the baby. Never purchase a kitten for a child unless you want one yourself. If you are elderly, it is only fair to consider what would happen to your cherished pet if it were to outlive you or if you were to become hospitalised for long periods.

It is most unfortunate that many people rush into the purchase of cats on an impulse. They then find they cannot cope if problems, and extra costs, ensue. Some lose interest in the pet once it matures past its kitten stage. The evidence of these realities is easily seen in the growing number of cats abandoned or taken to animal shelters every year. Invariably their owners will make feeble excuses for why the cat cannot be kept. But the bottom line is they did not stop to consider at the outset what responsible ownership entailed.

The Oriental Shorthair is not a

breed for those wishing for a quiet, rather independent, sort of breed. It needs things to do and people, or animal companions, to interact with. Denied these, it can be the worst sort of cat to own. It will find destructive things to occupy its mind and athletic capabilities. It may also become very stressed. This will increase the potential for a moody and unpredictable disposition to develop.

The Oriental Shorthair makes an excellent lap cat—more so than breeds such as the Persian. Its very short coat means it is able to sit on a lap without getting too hot, which will happen with a longhaired breed. Additionally, because of its constant playing and interaction with its owner, it develops a very strong bond. This increases its desire to enjoy the closest possible relationship with those who show it affection. For this reason, cats of the Siamese group are often considered the most dog-like of cats. They will respond more than most breeds to any form of training. The Oriental is a very vocal breed. It will continually chat or seek attention from its owner. Once again, this is a trait that will delight owners wanting a strong-bonding breed.

In its non-active mode, the Oriental is a quiet and very sensitive breed that enjoys nothing more than to be close to

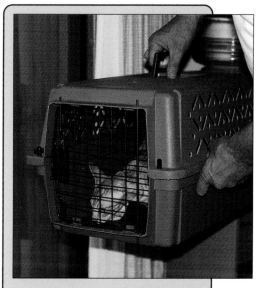

TAKING KITTY HOME
Arrange collection of the kitten as early in the day as possible. If a long journey is involved, be sure to take a few breaks so kitty does not suffer from travel sickness. Do not make stops to show the kitten to friends; this represents a health hazard. Once home, offer the kitten a drink, then allow it to sleep if it so requires. Children must be educated to handle a kitten gently, never to tease it and to respect its sleeping privacy. Until it is litter-trained it should be restricted to the kitchen or another room with an easy-to-clean floor surface.

its owner. Naturally it will want to share its owner's chair, bed and all other possessions. This, after all, is what being a true companion is all about.

Selecting a kitten from a healthy, well-bred litter guarantees a happier, more stable cat for the owner.

have developed the needed resistance to major diseases. They are more likely to become stressed by the premature removal from their mother and siblings. Their vaccinations will not be fully effective. These facts will dramatically increase the risk of immediate problems.

KITTEN OR ADULT?

Most potential owners normally want a kitten because it is so cute, cuddly and playful. A kitten is easily trained and has not yet developed bad habits, which the older Oriental Shorthair may have done. This said, if you plan to breed or exhibit, there are advantages in obtaining a young adult. Other potential owners, such as the elderly, may benefit by avoiding the demanding needs of a young kitten. In both of these instances, a good age is when the youngster is 9–15 months old. Even a fully mature Oriental Shorthair may prove an excellent choice for some owners.

Kittens should not be obtained under 12 weeks old, though 14–16 weeks is better. No reputable breeder will sell them younger than this. Less caring breeders will let them go to new homes as young as eight weeks of age. Such juveniles will barely have been weaned. They will not

SEX & COLOUR PATTERN

If it is to be purely a pet, the Oriental Shorthair's gender is unimportant. Both are delightful. Males are usually larger, bolder and more outgoing. Females tend to be more discerning about which humans they like. However, each Oriental Shorthair is an individual. Its character and health, more than its sex, should be the basis of selection. Again, the sex is unimportant for the potential exhibitor. It is not even necessary for the cat to be sexually 'entire.' Classes for neuters are featured in shows.

Those with breeding aspirations are advised to obtain only females. All pet owners should regard neutering (males) and spaying (females) as obligatory. Today this can be effected at any age after eight weeks.

The colour pattern is a matter of personal preference. It should never be placed ahead of health and character. Some colours and patterns will be more readily available than others will. The more popular varieties may be less costly than the rarer ones. This would generally not apply to prospective breeding or exhibition individuals, where type quality will be as important as colour or pattern.

LOOK BEFORE YOU LEAP

It is important that you view as many Oriental Shorthair kittens as you can. This gives you a good mental picture of what a healthy typical example should look like and cost for the quality and colour you want. Normally, you will get what you pay for. If you look for the cheapest kitten, there will be a sound reason why it is the cheapest!

The best place to start your search is a cat show. At large shows, most of the colour varieties will be on display. Purchase the show catalogue. It lists all the exhibitors and their addresses. You can see if any live in your immediate locality. Whenever possible, it is best to purchase locally so you can visit the home of the breeder. Some will insist you do so in order to be satisfied that you will make a good owner.

Shows and breeders are advertised in the various cat magazines available from newsagents. You can also contact a major cat registry. They will supply a list of national and regional clubs, which are usually able to supply breeder lists. When visiting a breeder, always make an appointment. Try to visit no more than one a day. This reduces the risk that you may transport pathogens (disease-causing organisms) from one establishment to the next. Selecting a good breeder is a case of noting the environment in which the cats are kept, the attitude of the owner to you and their cats, and how friendly and healthy the kittens look. It is vital the chosen kitty has an outgoing personality. It must not appear timid or very shy. This indicates a lack of breeder socialisation or a

HOMEMADE TOYS

Cats love to play and pet shops have many cat toys to choose from. Sometimes, however, people give their cats homemade toys. These can be harmful to your cat, as they could have pieces that could break off and be swallowed. Only give your pet toys from the pet shop that have been proven safe for cats.

The personality of the Oriental Shorthair should be friendly and outgoing. The temperament of the kitten's parents will have a direct impact on its personality.

genetic weakness in its temperament. Either way, it is not a kitten you should select.

CHOOSING A KITTEN

If you choose the breeder wisely, and especially if a friend recommends him, this will remove potential problems related to your making a poor choice. However, a little knowledge on what to look for will not go amiss. Observe the kittens from a distance to ensure none is unduly lethargic, which is never a good sign. If any display signs of illness, this should bring to an end any further thoughts of purchase from that source. A reputable breeder would not allow an ill kitten to remain within its litter.

It is always advisable to select a kitten that shows particular interest in you. Oriental Shorthairs are very discerning. If both of you are drawn to each other, this will greatly enhance the bonding essential for a strong relationship.

Once a particular kitten has been selected, it should be given a close physical inspection. The eyes and nose must show no signs of weeping or discharge. The ears will be erect and fresh-smelling. The coat should look healthy, never dry and dull. There must be no signs of parasites in the fur. There will be no bald areas of fur, nor bodily swellings or abrasions. Lift the tail and

A HEALTHY KITTEN
Closely inspect any kitten before making a final decision. Keep in mind the following points:
Eyes and nose: Clean and clear with no signs of discharge.
Ears: Fresh-smelling and erect.
Coat: Healthy, not dull or dry.
Anal region: Clean with no staining of the fur.
Feet: Four toes on each foot, plus a dewclaw on the inside of each front leg.
Teeth: Correct bite.
There should be no signs of parasites or bald areas of fur. A potbelly may indicate worms.

inspect the anal region. This must be clean, with no indication of congealed faecal matter. Any staining of the fur indicates current or recent diarrhoea.

The kitten must not display a potbelly. This may indicate worms or other internal disorders.

CAT LITTER

The litter that is used in cat boxes can be very variable, and in many cases cats reject the use of a cat box because of the litter. Certainly, if your cat rejects the use of the cat box, you should try different litters. You can start with the litters available at your local pet shop, then you can try sand, dirt, cedar shavings or whatever will appeal to your cat. Several cat owners grow clover in a tray and their cats seem to prefer that. However, the tray is kept outdoors and the cats may simply be marking the clover tray rather than using it for elimination purposes.

Check the teeth to be sure of a correct bite. Bear in mind that the jawbones do not develop at the same rate. Minor imperfections may correct themselves (they may also get worse), but major faults will not. Inspect the feet to see that there are four toes on each, plus a dewclaw on the inside of each front leg.

With respect to the colour, there is no link between this and health other than deafness in certain white varieties. Any faults in the colour or its quality will only be of importance in breeding or exhibition individuals. The potential breeder/exhibitor should obtain a copy of the official standard so he is *au fait* with all colour, pattern, and bodily faults of the breed.

KITTY SHOPPING SPREE

Certain accessories should be regarded as obligatory and obtained before the kitten arrives in your home.

SCRATCHING POST

This will save the furniture from being abused! There are many models, some being simple posts, while others are combined with play stations and sleeping quarters. These are the best.

LITTER BOX(ES)

Some are open trays; others are domed to provide extra privacy. Still others have special bases in which odour removers are fitted.

CAT LITTER

There are numerous types on the market, each offering advantages and drawbacks. Avoid the low-cost types that contain a lot of dangerous dust. Use those that are fully biodegradable.

Liners are available for most litter trays to assist in keeping them clean and more manageable.

Cat carriers are a necessity of cat ownership, and no cat welcomes the opportunity of being carted about in a crate. Nonetheless, the carrier is the only safe option for transport to the veterinary surgeon.

Double-bowl feeders are very convenient for feeding your cat. Go to your pet shop to purchase top-quality feeders, which should come in a variety of colours, styles and sizes.

Purchasing a scratching post is a smart option for the cat owner. It's best to purchase a sturdy, well-made post that will last your cat years of utility.

There is nothing glamorous about purchasing a litter box, yet cat owners have few options in this regard. Consult your local pet shop to see a selection of boxes. Some cats do not accept a covered box, while others welcome the 'privacy.'

If you are considering walking your Oriental, you must have a lead that is suitable for a cat.

Clipping the Oriental's claws requires instruction, practice and a suitable tool. Start clipping the claws as soon as you have the kitten at home.

FOOD/WATER DISHES

Polished metal has the longest wear life. Earthenware is less costly than metal and superior to the plastic types.

GROOMING TOOLS

These will comprise a good-quality bristle brush, a fine-toothed comb, nail trimmers, and a soft chamois leather.

CAT COLLAR AND/OR HARNESS

Select elasticised collars. Be sure a name and address disc or barrel is fitted to this. A harness must be a snug but comfortable fit if it is to be effective.

ADOPTING AN ADULT

Some owners, such as the elderly, may benefit by adopting an adult cat. They can avoid the demanding needs of a young kitten and enjoy the advantages of a well-trained adult, making grooming an easier task. Breeders and exhibitors can also benefit from purchasing an older cat because it is easier to assess the quality. Sometimes, though, older cats can have bad habits that are hard to break. So if you are thinking about obtaining an older cat, it is important to thoroughly investigate possible behavioural and health problems.

Stainless steel dishes for food and water are the best and longest lasting.

CAT-CARRYING BOX

This is essential for transporting the cat to the vet or other places, as well as for home restriction when needed. Be sure it is large enough to accommodate a fully-grown Oriental Shorthair, not just a kitten. The choice is between collapsible models, soft plastic types and, the best choice, those made of fibreglass.

Your local pet shop should carry a full range of litter trays, litter boxes and the tools with which you keep the box clean.

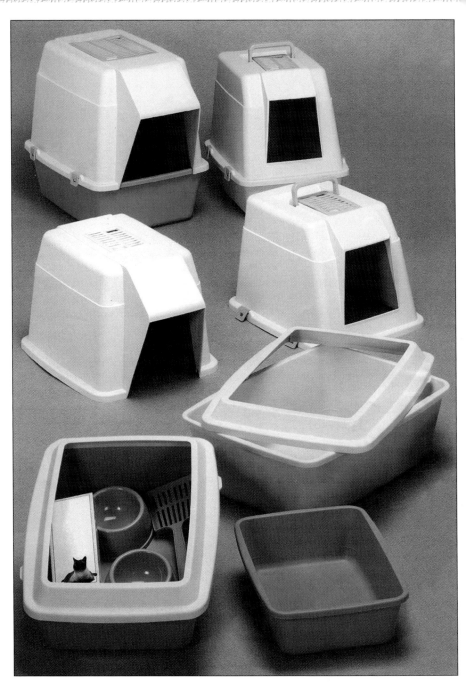

Your local pet shop should have an array of scratching posts that will delight your Oriental. Do not attempt to make a post yourself as many carpets are too weak to stand the tearing or may have been dyed with chemicals harmful to cats.

Like all athletic Orientals, the Havana is inquisitive and agile, making the cat a challenge to keep safe and out of harm's way.

For a kitten, a human environment holds many dangers. Its owner must protect it from these until it becomes agile and wiser. The following dangers lurk in typical households. Always check whether there are additional ones in your home. The most important decision you need to make from the outset is whether or not the kitten is to be given outdoor liberty.

HOW MUCH FREEDOM?

More than at any time in the past, the question of how much freedom a cat should be given is the subject of heated debate. It is a very subjective matter. Here the more pertinent points are given so you can relate these to your home location. This, to a very large degree, should influence your decision.

Cats living in or close to an urban area are at the highest safety risk. The amount of traffic is such that death from road accidents is a major concern. In such environments there are high dog populations, some of

BE ONE JUMP AHEAD

Seemingly innocuous things, such as doors, can become life-threatening should they suddenly slam shut on a kitten due to a strong draught. When windows and external doors are open, be sure internal doors are secured with a doorstop. At all times be one jump ahead of a kitten in terms of identifying dangerous situations.

which are feral. Injury or death from dog attacks is therefore another major source of danger to a feline.

Urban cat populations are also extremely high. Far too many cats are living a virtually feral existence. These are tough, street-wise cats that often carry fleas and other parasites that are vectors of disease. Some will be carriers of, or infected with, feline leukaemia and other deadly diseases.

The typical feline family pet can be badly injured if it becomes engaged in fights with these roaming bullies. Furthermore, their very presence in and around a gentle cat's garden can cause the pet severe stress. This can make it fearful of stepping outside its home. In some instances, it may cause the pet to actually leave its home.

Sadly, if these risks are not enough, there is no shortage of people who will steal a

Many cats are attracted to running water, which can pose dangers for the Oriental and owner alike. It is wise to discourage cats from exploring bathrooms and kitchens.

THE GARAGE AND SHED

These two buildings are very dangerous to a kitten. Sharp and heavy tools, nails, glass jars, garden weed killers and open tins of paint are but a sampling of the items the average family uses or stores in these. A kitten may clamber into the engine compartment of a vehicle. This could be fatal if the owner happened to start the engine before the kitten had removed itself. Always know where the kitten is.

pedigreed cat, the more so if it is friendly. Add to this the number of abusive people who do not like cats roaming into their gardens, and the scenario is not good. Finally, free-roaming cats also take a heavy toll on local bird and wildlife populations.

Taking these various facts into account, the urban cat is best kept indoors. It can enjoy the benefit of the outdoors if supplied with a roomy aviary-type exercise pen. Some cats can be trained to walk on a lead. This allows outdoor enjoyment, even if this is restricted to the garden. When walking your cat in public places, use only a harness. This is much safer than a collar.

In contrast to urban situations, the cat living in a rural environment is far safer, the more so if there are no immediate neighbours or busy roads. Even so, it is wise to restrict the cat's outdoor freedom to daylight hours. During the night it is more likely to get run over or to threaten local wildlife.

Those living between the extremes of isolated areas and busy urban environments should consider the local risk factor. Generally, it is best to keep the cat indoors but to provide an outdoor exercise pen.

HOUSEHOLD DANGERS

Within its home, a kitten is best viewed as an accident waiting to happen! The most dangerous room is the kitchen. Hot electric hobs, naked flames from gas rings, boiling pans of food or water and sinks full of water are obvious hazards. An iron left on

THE TRAVELLING CAT

Whenever your cat needs to be taken on a car journey, never let it travel loose in the vehicle, which is illegal. It must always be in its carrying box. If a cat were to go under the clutch or brake pedal when the car was moving, this would be dangerous to all occupants. A cat might also spring from one seat to another, which might distract the driver. This could have disastrous results.

Never leave a cat alone in a car on a hot day. The temperature can rise dramatically to the point that the cat is unable to breathe. It could die of heat stroke. Always leave a window partially open, but not so wide that the agile cat could escape.

BOARDING YOUR CAT

Cats do not like to travel and the best alternative is to have a trusted friend, relative or pet-sitter watch your cat in your home. If this is impossible, then you may have to board your cat. You can get recommendations from friends or your veterinary surgeon as to which catteries are reputable. When choosing a boarding house, you should visit the facility beforehand to make certain that it is clean and quiet, and that the personnel are caring and attentive to boarders. You should also enquire about their policies concerning health, vaccinations and neutering.

its board with cable trailing to the floor is an invitation to a kitten to jump up—with potentially fatal consequences. Washing machines or spin dryers with warm clothes in them, and their doors open, are

Kittens can get into trouble during their investigations. While getting electrocuted is always a concern, they more usually cause damage to delicate items.

OTHER DANGERS

Other potential dangers are when electric tools are left lying about and connected to power outlets—even worse if they are left on, as with bench saws. If the kitten is given freedom to exercise in a garden containing a pond, the kitten must be under constant supervision. Cherished ornaments should be placed out of reach of the kitten, as much for their safety as for any danger they may present to the kitty. It's not always the direct danger of something that can be the problem. If an ornament or similar item crashes to the floor, this can startle the kitten into a panicked departure! The kitten could then fall from a shelf in its haste.

inviting places to nap. Always check that the kitty isn't inside if the door has been left open. Cupboards containing poisonous or other dangerous substances should always be kept securely closed.

In the living room, the normal dangers are aquariums without hoods, unguarded fires, electric bar heaters, poisonous indoor plants, trailing electrical wires and ornaments that may be knocked over by a mischievous kitty. Toilets can be fatal to an over-curious kitten. The same is true of a bath containing water. Balconies should be safeguarded to remove the potential for the kitten to slip and fall.

DANGEROUS DISINFECTANTS

Although owners should disinfect the litter box regularly to prevent disease and illness, some household disinfectants can be harmful to cats. Pine-oil-based cleaners are toxic to cats. DO NOT use them. Products containing Phenol should also be avoided. Bleach is a good disinfectant to use; however, be sure to rinse the litter box thoroughly and air it out to get rid of any fumes.

As ornamental as the Oriental may be, it must still be kept out of trouble in the home and out.

Today the feeding of cats has been reduced to its most simple level with the availability of many scientifically prepared commercial diets. However, this fact can result in owners' becoming casual in their approach to the subject. While the main object of a given diet is to provide the ingredients that promote healthy growth and maximum immunity to disease, it also fulfils an important secondary role.

A proper diet must maintain in the cat a psychological feeling of well-being that avoids nutritionally related stress

HIGH-QUALITY FOOD
The value of a cat food is determined by its protein/carbohydrate compositions. High-quality foods will contain more protein. The cat is a prime predator and needs a high proportion of protein in its diet.

problems or syndromes. By ensuring the diet is balanced, of good variety, and never monotonous, these dual roles will be achieved. This approach will also avoid the situation of the cat's becoming a finicky eater.

BALANCE AND VARIETY
A balanced diet means one that contains all of the major ingredients—protein, fats, carbohydrates, vitamins and minerals—in the ratios needed to ensure maximum growth and health. Variety means supplying foods in a range of forms that will maintain and stimulate the cat's interest in its meals. Commercially formulated foods come in three levels of moisture: low (dried), semi-moist and moist (tinned foods).

Generally, the dried and moist

MILK AND CATS
Milk, although associated with cats, is not needed once kittenhood has passed. Indeed, excess can create skeletal and other problems. Some cats may become quite ill if given too much. They are unable to digest its lactose content. However, small amounts may be appreciated as a treat. Goat's milk, diluted condensed milk and low-lactose milks are better than cow's milk.

forms are more popular. Dried cat foods have the advantage that they can be left in the cat dish for longer periods of time than tinned foods. They are ideal for supplying on a free-choice basis. Like the tinned varieties, they come in a range of popular flavours.

In order to meet the specific needs of a kitten, there are specially formulated foods available. These contain the higher protein levels needed by a growing kitten. As it grows, the kitten can be slowly weaned onto the adult types. There are also special brands available from vets for any kitten or cat that may have a dietary problem as well as special diets for the older cat. These may need lower ratios of certain ingredients, such as proteins and sodium, so as to reduce the workload of the liver.

Flavours should be rotated so that interest in meals is maintained. This also encourages familiarity with different tastes. Naturally, Oriental Shorthair cats will display a greater liking for certain flavours and brands than for others.

FRESH FOODS

To add greater variety and interest, there are many fresh foods that Oriental Shorthairs enjoy. Some will be very helpful in cleaning the teeth and exercising jaw muscles. All have

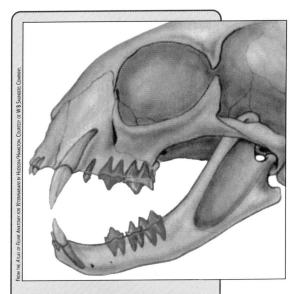

FROM THE *ATLAS OF FELINE ANATOMY FOR VETERINARIANS* BY HUDSON/HAMILTON. COURTESY OF W. B. SAUNDERS COMPANY.

MEET THE MEAT-EATERS

Since cats are carnivorous, their teeth are designed to bite and cut. Except for crunching dried foods, cats do very little chewing. They have the fewest teeth of any common domestic mammal—typically 30 (although there are some variations). The canines usually are more developed than the incisors.

the benefit of providing different textures and smells that help stimulate the palate. Feed these foods two or three times a week as treats or occasionally as complete meals.

Cooked poultry, including the skin, but minus the bones, is usually a favourite, as is quality raw or cooked mincemeat. Cooked

IMPORTANT DON'TS

- Do not let your cat become a fussy eater. Cats are not born fussy but are made that way by their owners. Your cat will not starve if given the correct food, but it may try to convince you otherwise. However, a cat that refuses all foods offered may be ill. Contact your vet.
- Do not give a cat sweet and sticky foods. These provide no benefit and, if eaten, will negatively affect normal appetite for wholesome foods.
- Do not feed vitamin and mineral supplements to either kittens or adults unless under advice from a veterinary surgeon. Excess vitamins and minerals can be as bad for your cat's health as a lack of them. They will create potentially dangerous cellular metabolic imbalances.
- Do not give any questionable foods, such as those that smell or look 'off.' If in doubt, discard them. Always store foods in cool, darkened cupboards. Be sure all foods from the freezer and refrigerator are fully thawed.

beef on the bone gives the cat something to enjoy. Cooked white fish, as well as tinned tuna or sardines, is an example of an ocean delight. Never feed raw fish; this can prove dangerous, even fatal. Although cats rarely enjoy items such as rice, pasta or cooked vegetables, these can, nonetheless, be finely chopped and mixed with meats or fish. Some Oriental Shorthairs may develop a taste for them. Various cheeses and scrambled or boiled eggs will often be appreciated—but never give raw eggs.

If the diet is balanced and varied, the addition of vitamin and mineral supplements is unnecessary and can actually prove dangerous. While certain of these compounds are released from the body if in excess, others are not. They are stored and can adversely affect efficient metabolism. If a cat shows loss of condition and disinterest in its food, discuss its diet with a vet.

HOW MUCH TO FEED

Food intake is influenced by many factors. These are the cat's age, activity level, the ambient temperature (more is eaten in the colder months), the cat's breeding state (rearing kittens) and the quality of the food. Always follow the breeder's recommendations on diet until your kitten has settled into your home. Thereafter the needed quantity will increase as

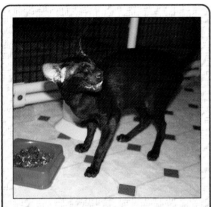

DIETARY DIFFERENCES BETWEEN CATS AND DOGS

You should never feed your cat dog food because dogs and cats have different dietary needs. Cats have a much higher need for fats than dogs, and kittens need more than adult cats. Cats also require unusually high levels of dietary protein as compared with those required by dogs. The foods you choose for your cat must supply these essential components.

ESTABLISHING DAILY INTAKE

Quoting amounts needed is impossible because of the varying factors mentioned. The best way to establish requirements is on an actual consumption basis. Place a small amount of food on the dish and see how quickly this is eaten. If all is devoured within a few minutes, add a little more. Repeat this until the kitten/cat is satiated and walks away from its dish. Do likewise at the other meals and you will quickly establish daily intake.

While the Oriental is a slender breed, owners must be sure that the cat is receiving a complete and balanced diet.

the kitten gets older, until full maturity at about two to three years of age.

As a basic guide, a four-month-old kitten will require four meals a day. At six months old, one meal can be dropped. By twelve months of age, only two meals will be required, possibly only one if dried foods are also available on a free-choice basis. As the number of meals is decreased, the quantity must be increased at the others.

DRIED FOOD— MORE WATER

If the cat is only given dried foods, it is essential that its water bowl is always full; it will need to drink more. But it is best to give both dried and moist food types. This minimises the risk of urological problems created by pH alkalinity associated with dried diets.

FOOD AND WATER CONTAINERS

Oriental Shorthair cats are not too fussy over what vessels are used for supplying their food and water, but a few tips are useful. Oriental Shorthair do not like to eat from dirty dishes any more than you would. The food bowl should be washed after each meal. Water containers should be washed and replenished every day. Saucers make ideal food plates. Wide feeders from your pet shop are excellent for dried biscuits. Pot or polished metal containers are better buys than plastic. They last longer and are easier to keep clean.

The Oriental Shorthair does not like to place its head into deep food dishes nor do they like their whiskers to touch the inner walls. Ensure dishes are wide and shallow.

WHERE AND WHEN TO FEED

Usually, the best place to feed a cat is in the kitchen. It is important to place food and water dishes as far away from the litter tray as possible. This could otherwise deter the cat from eating. Cats also like to eat in quiet comfort. Meals should be spread across the entire day. When the number of meals is reduced to two, these should be given in the morning and evening at convenient times. For the Oriental Shorthair given outdoor freedom, it is best to feed the main meal in the evening. This encourages it to come home at this time. It can then be kept indoors overnight.

EAT YOUR HAIRBALLS AWAY

Food companies have developed formulas containing a wholesome fibre blend that moves ingested hair through the cat's digestive tract, thus minimising the occurrence of hairballs. Tests show that feeding these formulas moved 80% more hair through the digestive tract, meaning fewer hairballs!

Choose your cats' dining location with care. If you share your home with dogs as well as cats, you might consider feeding the cats on an elevated surface (to deter canine sampling).

From the perspective of grooming, the Oriental Shorthair has an easy non-matting coat. If brushed every day, it will rarely need combing, though this is beneficial. Brisk brushing followed by a polish, using a chamois leather or piece of silk cloth, will maintain the fur in super condition. If you frequently stroke your Oriental Shorthair, the natural oils on your hand will give the coat a sleek look.

Among the most common cat problems is ear mites. Have your veterinary surgeon examine your Oriental for presence of mites or debris. Treatment is simple once detection is certain.

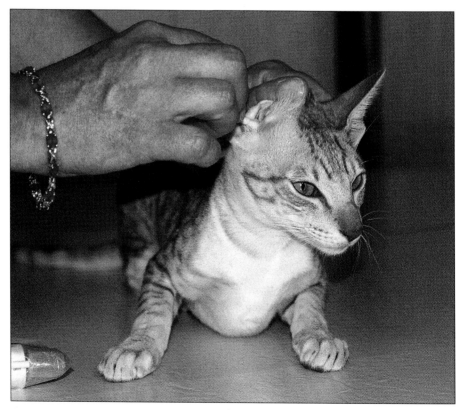

Regular grooming also enables close examination of the cat for any signs of problems. These include fleas or mites, small wounds, abrasions, swellings and bald areas. The grooming process should include inspection of the cat's ears, teeth and nails.

BRUSHING

Place the cat on a table of a height enabling you to comfortably control and groom the kitty. It can be useful to place white paper on the table. If any fleas are present, you will more easily notice them if they are groomed out of the fur. If the grooming is carried out gently, cats enjoy the experience. You should start when your Oriental Shorthair is still a kitten.

Commence by brushing the fur on the back of the neck. Work along the back and down the sides, then down the legs and finally the tail. The abdominal area must be brushed more gently as it is very sensitive.

Next, repeat the process using the fine-toothed comb. Then comb against the lie of the hair. This will enable you to see if there are any parasites present. These often favour the tail base or the neck behind the ears. Next comb with the lie of the fur. Add a final lustre by brushing with the chamois.

GROOMING EQUIPMENT

For total grooming needs, the following are required:
1. Semi-stiff bristle brush or rubber-pinned brush
2. Fine-toothed comb
3. Flea comb
4. Thin chamois leather and/or a silken cloth
5. Pair of guillotine-type nail trimmers
6. Medium-soft toothbrush
7. Cat toothpaste
8. Supply of cotton wool and cotton buds
9. Bottle of baby oil

BATHING

Occasionally, even shorthaired cats may need bathing. This may be of the wet or dry type. For wet baths, using the kitchen sink is preferable to a bath. This saves bending and allows for better control of the cat. To prevent the cat from sliding, use a rubber mat. A spray attachment is more efficient than a jug to wet and rinse the coat. The cat should have its own towels.

The choice of shampoo is important. It should ideally be

HAIRBALLS (Trichobezoar)

When cats self-groom, they invariably swallow some of their hairs. Normally these do not create a problem. However, if many dead hairs are in the coat, these may be licked and swallowed to accumulate in the stomach as hairballs. These are more common in longhaired breeds than in those with short hair. Hairballs may create intestinal blockages that may so irritate the cat's intestinal tract that it vomits the hairball or voids it via its faecal matter.

If the hairball is not removed, and the cat displays reduced appetite, veterinary assistance is needed. Regular grooming greatly reduces the risk of this condition. Additionally, a teaspoon of liquid paraffin or other laxative once a week may be helpful in cats prone to this problem. A laxative, however, is unlikely to remove an existing hairball. Pineapple juice containing the enzyme bromelain may break down small furballs. One teaspoonful a day for three days is the recommended dosage.

DRY SHAMPOO

A dry bath may be preferred to a wet one during very cold weather or when the cat is not well enough for a water bath. Sprinkle dry shampoo into the coat and give it a good brushing. This will remove excess grease and dirt without being as thorough as a wet bath. Be very sure all the powder is brushed from the fur to avoid potential irritation and consequential scratching.

formulated for cats—do not use one for dogs. This could cause problems on a cat's coat. Baby shampoos are the best alternative. Dry shampoos in powder form are available from pet shops. Alternatives would be talcum powder, powdered chalk or heated bran flakes.

The kitten should be bathed by the time it is six months of age. This will familiarise it with the process before it matures and the process degenerates into a pitched battle. Cats have no love of bathing but can come to accept it if it does not become an unpleasant ordeal.

Grooming should always precede bathing, as this will remove any dead hairs. The key to success lies in ensuring that no water or shampoo is allowed to enter and irritate the eyes or ears. You should be able to cope single-handedly with a kitten. However, it may be prudent to have someone else present just in case the adult proves more of a super cat than a kitten!

The water temperature should be warm, never cold or too hot. Prepare a shampoo and water solution before commencing. Have a large towel at hand. Commence by soaking the fur of the neck, then work along the back, sides, legs and tail. Pour shampoo onto the back and work this in all directions until the cat has been fully shampooed. Next, thoroughly rinse all the shampoo away. It is essential that none be left, otherwise it may cause later irritation. Gently but firmly squeeze all water from the coat. The face can be cleaned using a dampened flannel.

Wrap the kitten in the towel and give it a brisk rubbing until it is as dry as possible. It can then be allowed to dry naturally, after which it can be given a final brush and polish. If the cat is normally allowed outdoors, do not allow this for some hours until you are sure

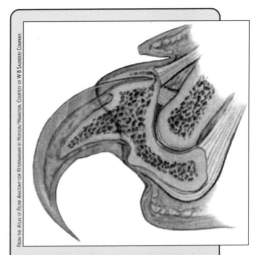

FROM THE ATLAS OF FELINE ANATOMY FOR VETERINARIANS BY HUDSON/HAMILTON, COURTESY OF W B SAUNDERS COMPANY.

DECLAWING

Declawing is the surgical removal of all of the claw (or nail) and the first toe joint. This practice is heavily frowned upon and even illegal in some countries, such as the United Kingdom.

Unfortunately, in some areas of the world this procedure is still performed. Some owners only have the claws from the front feet removed; others do all four feet. An alternative surgical procedure is removing the tendon that allows the cat to protract its claws. This procedure, referred to as a tendonectomy, as compared to an onychectomy (removal of the claws), is less traumatic for the cat. Claws still must be filed and trimmed after a tendonectomy.

Declawing is not always 100% successful. In two-thirds of the cases, the cats recovered in 72 hours. Only 4–5% of the cats hadn't recovered within a fortnight. About 3% of the cats had their claws grow back!

CLEAN CATS

Cats are self-groomers. They use their barbed tongues and front paws for grooming. Some cats never groom themselves, while others spend up to a third of their waking hours grooming themselves. Licking stimulates certain skin glands that make the coat waterproof.

the coat is dry. In the colder months, it is best to attend to bathing in the early evening and keep the cat indoors overnight. The use of a hand dryer is not essential on a short-coated breed, but does shorten the drying time.

EARS, EYES AND NAILS

When inspecting the ears, look for any signs of dirt. This can be gently wiped away using a dampened cotton bud or one with just a little baby or vegetable oil on it. Never attempt to probe into the ear. If the ear is very waxed, this may indicate any of various health problems. A visit to the vet is recommended. The corner of the eyes can be gently wiped with damp cotton wool to remove any dust that occasionally accumulates.

Inspection of a cat's claws is achieved by firstly restraining it while on its back on your lap or held against your chest. Hold the paw and apply pressure to the top of this with your thumb. The nail will appear from its sheath. If the nail needs trimming, use the appropriate trimmers.

It is vital you do not cut into, or even too close to, the quick, which is a blood vessel. This can be seen as a darker area of the nail in pink-clawed cats. It is more difficult, or not possible, to see the quick in dark-coloured nails. In such instances, trim less. You may need a helper to do the trimming or the holding. If in

HAIR GROWTH

Cat's body hairs grow from the follicles, which are connected to the dermis. Tactile hairs (whiskers) are thicker and longer, originating three times deeper than the normal body hairs.

doubt, let your vet do this for you. If cats have ample access to scratching posts, they will only infrequently, if ever, require their nails to be trimmed.

HAIR, HAIR EVERYWHERE!

Cat's hairs grow denser on the abdomen than on the back. The hairs grow according to both light periodicity (daylight versus dark nights) and temperature. Outdoor cats living in colder climates cast their coats twice a year, in the spring and fall, while house cats do so all year long.

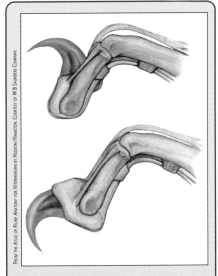

FROM THE ATLAS OF FELINE ANATOMY FOR VETERINARIANS BY HUDSON/HAMILTON. COURTESY OF W B SAUNDERS COMPANY.

RETRACTABLE CLAWS

When at rest, a cat's claws are retracted. The muscles hold the claws in their sheaths. The claw is then extended if the cat wishes to attack prey, defend itself, grab an object or climb. That is why your cat's claws are not always visible. This is true for all species of felines except the cheetah, which is unable to retract its claws, except when it is very young.

TEETH

From its youngest days, your kitten should become familiar with having its teeth cleaned. Many owners do not give their cats' teeth the attention they should. This has become progressively more important due to the soft-diet regimens of modern cats. Initially, gently rub the kitten's teeth using a soft cloth on which toothpaste has been placed. This will accustom the kitten to having its teeth touched as well as to the taste of the tooth cleaner. When this is no problem for the kitten, you can progress to a soft toothbrush and ultimately one of medium hardness. Periodically, let your vet check the cat's mouth.

Once accustomed to nail clipping, your Oriental Shorthair should tolerate the procedure with patience. Some cats despise humans' touching their feet, and these will require an extra pair of arms to handle.

GINGIVITIS (Plasmocytic-Lymphocytic Stomatitis)

There are many causes of this condition. But the end result is the same—bad breath, excessive plaque, tooth loss and, almost certainly, pain. The cat salivates excessively, starts to eat less and consequently loses weight. On inspection, the gums are swollen, especially in the area of the premolar and molar teeth. They bleed easily. There are various treatments, such as antibiotics, immunostimulants and disinfectant mouth gels. However, these invariably prove short-term and merely delay the inevitable treatment of extraction.

Prevention avoids this painful condition. Regular tooth inspection and cleaning, plus provision of hard-food items, such as cat biscuits, achieve this to a large extent. There are also special cat chews made of dried fish that help clean the teeth. They also contain antibacterial enzymes that minimise or prevent secondary bacteria from accumulating. Ask for these at your pet shop or vet's surgery. Gingivitis may commence in kittens, so do not think it is something that only occurs in older cats.

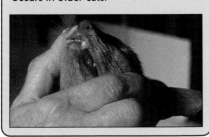

A well-trained Oriental will allow you to brush its teeth. Introduce the cat to the teeth-cleaning process gradually and eventually it will accept the brush.

PRESS-ON NAILS!

A stylish and fairly successful inhibitor of scratching is to use a plastic covering on the nails. A plastic sheath is placed over each nail and glued on with a strong, permanent adhesive. Depending upon the cat's activity, these sheaths last from one to three months.

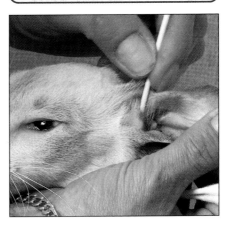

Probing into a cat's ears with a cotton bud is not recommended as a sudden jerk from the cat can cause damage to its ear.

While training an adult cat is rather trying, a kitten accepts instruction quite readily. Provide stability and respect for the kitten and it will respond nicely to your training efforts.

SETTING THE GROUND RULES

From the outset you must determine the ground rules and stick to them. Always remember that your companion's patterns of behaviour begin to form from the moment it first arrives at your home. If the future adult is not to be given outdoor freedom, then do not let it outdoors as a kitten. If any rooms are to be out of bounds to the adult, then do not let the kitten into them. Stability is vital in a cat's life; without it, the result will be stress and its related behavioural changes.

Ground rules of how to handle the kitten and to respect its privacy when sleeping should be instilled into all children. The cat's meals should be given at about the same time each day. This will have the secondary advantage that the pet's toilet habits will be more predictable.

One of the outstanding virtues of cats is that they are easy to live with. They are fastidious in their personal habits related to grooming and toilet routines and basically require very little of their owners. Nonetheless, behavioural problems in cats can occur, and an owner needs to understand all the possible causes and solutions. You may never encounter a single problem with your cat, but it pays to be prepared should your feline charge disrupt your domestic bliss.

THE BASIS OF TRAINING

The most effective means of training a cat is via reinforcement of success. A cat learning from lavish praise of doing what is required will want to repeat the action to gain more affection. There are no potential negative side effects. Conversely, when scolding or other methods of discipline are used, there is always the possibility that the cat will not relate the punishment to what the owner had intended.

For example, you cannot discipline for something done in the past. The past is anything much longer than a few minutes

WHY WHISKERS?
Cats are famous for their whiskers. The whiskers are tactile hairs by which cats feel. Most tactile hairs are on the cat's face, mostly on the upper lip and around the eyes, and on the wrist (carpus). These carpal hairs are extremely sensitive and are found on many predatory animals that use their front paws for holding their victims.

ago. If you call the cat to you and punish it for something done hours earlier, it cannot relate to that action. It will relate the discipline to the act of going to you when called! This will create insecurity in the pet, increasing the risk that more problems will develop.

REMEDIAL METHODS
When faced with a problem, firstly try to pinpoint the likely cause(s). Next, consider the remedial options. Be sure these will not result in negative side effects linked to you. Always be the

paragon of patience. Some problems may be extremely complex and deeply rooted within the cat's behaviour patterns. As such, they are habits not easily changed, and often difficult to analyse. In discussing the following problems it is hoped you will understand the basic ways in which to correct other unwanted patterns of behaviour that might occur. But always remember it is far better to avoid a problem than to correct it.

THE LITTER TRAY
A very common problem for some owners is that their cat starts to attend to its toileting needs anywhere other than in its litter tray. The problem may become apparent from the time the kitten gets to its new home, or it may develop at any time during its life. So, let us start from the beginning

THE TRUTH ABOUT CATS AND DOGS
Cats are unique in having the scrotum fully haired, a marked difference from their canine counterparts. This led one early observer to say that cats were not small dogs! Dogs were domesticated well before cats since cats only served to protect the abode of the owner from rodents, while dogs served as guards, hunters, herders, exterminators and as loyal companions that were readily trainable. Cats have always been more independent and less trainable.

and try to avoid the situation.

Until you are satisfied that the kitten is using its litter tray consistently, do not give it access to carpeted rooms. The youngster should already have been litter-trained well before you obtained it. You should obtain a litter tray similar to the one it is already familiar with. It is also important that the same brand of litter is used, at least initially. Place the tray in a quiet spot so the kitten has privacy when attending to its needs.

A kitten will need to relieve itself shortly after it has eaten, exercised or been sleeping. Watch it carefully at these times. If it stoops to attend to its needs other than in the litter tray, calmly lift it into its tray and scratch at the litter. Never shout or panic the kitty by making a sudden rush for it. If it does what is hoped, give it lots of praise. If it steps out of the tray, gently place it back in for a few seconds.

If nothing happens, be patient and wait, then repeat the process. If it fouls the floor when you are not watching, simply clean this up and wait for the next opportunity to transport the kitten to its tray. It rarely takes long for a kitten to consistently use this. Be very sure the tray is kept spotless. Cats have no more desire to use a fouled toilet than you do. Every few days, give the cat tray a good wash. Use soapy water and always rinse it

thoroughly. Allow it to dry, then fill the tray with litter to depth of about 1.5–2 inches.

By identifying the cause(s) of litter-box problems, the correction is often self-evident. However, once the cause has been corrected, this is only part of the solution. Next, the habit of fouling other places must be overcome. Where possible, do not let the cat enter rooms in which it has started to foul until the odour has had time to fully disperse. Wash the area of the fouling, then treat carpets and soft furnishings with an odour neutraliser (not an air freshener)

CATS AND OTHER PETS

If you already have a pet cat or cats, or dogs, or almost any other animal that isn't small, creeping or crawling, your cat can usually be socialised so the other pet and the cat will tolerate each other. In many cases, cats and dogs become quite friendly and attached to each other, often making frequent physical contacts, sleeping together or even sharing each other's food.

CAUSES OF LITTER-BOX PROBLEMS

1. The litter tray is dirty. Cats never like to use a previously fouled tray.
2. The litter has been changed to one of a different texture that the cat does not like. Generally the finer-grained litters are the most favoured.
3. A scented litter is being used to mask odours. The cat may not like the scent. Such litters should not be necessary if the tray is regularly cleaned.
4. The tray is regularly cleaned, but an ammonium or pine-based disinfectant is being used. This may aggravate the cat's sensitive nasal mucous membranes. Additionally, the phenols in pine are dangerous to cats.
5. The litter tray is located too close to the cat's food and water bowls. Cats do not like to eat near litter trays or to defecate/urinate close to their feeding areas.
6. Another cat or free-roaming pet has been added to the household and is causing the cat stress. In multi-cat households, two or more trays may be needed.
7. There is insufficient litter in the tray. There should be about 2 inches of litter depth.
8. The cat has developed a fear of using the tray due to an upsetting experience. For instance, the owner may have caught the cat as it finished using the tray in order that it could be given a medicine. Children may be disturbing it while it is relieving itself.
9. The cat is ill (or elderly) and is unable to control its bowel movements. Veterinary attention is required.
10. The cat, because of one or more of the previous problems, has established other more favourable areas.

from your pet shop or vet.

If the cat cannot be prevented from entering certain rooms, then cover previously fouled areas with plastic sheeting or tinfoil, or rinse the area with white vinegar. Also, place a litter tray in the fouled room while the retraining is underway. It may help if a different size, type or colour of tray is used.

SCENT MARKING
Both sexes scent mark, though males are more prolific. It is a means of advertising their presence in a territory, thus an integral part of their natural behaviour. Spraying is usually done against a vertical surface. It tells other males

MARKING TERRITORY

Cats are geographical by nature and they mark their territories in the usual way...by spraying their urine. The frequency of spraying is amazing! A non-breeding male cat that is not within its own turf will spray about 13 times an hour while travelling through the new territory. A breeding male will spray almost twice as much. One reports states that free-ranging males spray 62.6 times an hour—that's more than once a minute!

Cat urine is recognisable for at least 24 hours and male cats spend a lot of time sniffing the area. Females spend less time, but both sexes easily recognise the urine from male cats that are strange to the area.

that the individual is residing in that territory. Alternatively, it will tell a female that a male lives close by—or it will tell the male that a female is in the area. It is thus a very important part of a cat's social language.

Neutered cats have little need to mark their territory, or leave their 'calling card' to attract mates. They are far less likely to spray than those not altered. However, scent marking may commence when the cat is attempting to assert its position in the household.

To overcome the problem of scent marking, the first need is to try to identify if there is an obvious specific cause. In multi-cat households, it also requires positive identification of the sprayer(s) and the favoured spraying surface. Try giving the cat more freedom and its own sleeping place, if it does not have one. Covering the sprayed surface with plastic sheeting, or a cloth impregnated with a scent the cat does not like (such as lemon, pepper or bleach), may be successful. Spraying the cat with a water pistol when catching it in the action is a common ploy. Veterinary treatment with the hormone progesterone may prove effective—discuss this with your vet.

SCRATCHING

Scratching is a normal feline characteristic. Unfortunately, house cats tend to destroy

CAUSES OF SCENT MARKING

1. Another cat, or pet, has been introduced to the household. It may be bullying the resident cat. This problem may resolve itself when the two get to know each other. The more cats there are, the longer it may take for the situation to be resolved. Much will depend on the space within which the cats may roam and whether they are able to avoid those they dislike.
2. The birth of a new family member may annoy the cat for a while, especially if its owner suddenly gives it less attention.
3. A friend staying in the home for a few days may not like cats. If 'shooed' away a number of times, the cat may feel it should assert its position and mark it.
4. If the cat is given outdoor freedom, a bully may have moved into the territory. Having lost control of its own garden, the pet may assert its territorial boundaries within its home. If a cat flap is used, another cat may be entering the home and this will trigger the resident to scent mark.

SCRATCHING FURNITURE

All cats need to scratch in order to maintain their claws in good condition. For this reason, one or more scratching posts strategically placed in the cat's most-used rooms will normally prevent the problem. Place the post in front of the scratched furniture. It can be moved steadily further away once the furniture is ignored. This is a problem that may become more manifest when cats are not allowed outdoors and have insufficient indoor provisions to scratch.

furniture to satisfy their need to scratch. Feral or outdoor cats usually attack a tree because trees are readily accessible and the bark of the tree suits their needs perfectly. If the outdoor cat lives in a pride, it will scratch more than a solitary feral cat. The reasons for this are known. When cats scratch, they leave tell-tale marks. Parts of

the nail's sheath exudate from glands located between their claws, and the visual aspects are the marks which cats leave to impress

THE PICA SYNDROME

The term 'pica' is a veterinary term that refers to a morbid desire to ingest things that are abnormal to the cat's diet. Cats are often addicted to soft materials like wool, silk, cotton or a mixture of these and synthetic cloths. Hard plastics, wood and even metals have been involved in this pica syndrome. If you observe your cat chewing these fabrics or materials, speak to your vet. Most vets who observe the pica syndrome think it is a nervous problem that can successfully be treated with drugs normally used for depression. In any case, the genetic makeup of your cat should be investigated and if pica occurs in any of the parents or previous offspring, do not breed your cat.

or advertise their presence.

Cat owners whose cats scratch should not consider the scratching as an aggressive behavioural disorder. It is normal for cats to scratch. Keeping your cat's claws clipped or filed so they are as short as possible, without causing bleeding, may inhibit scratching. Your vet can teach you how to do this. Clipping and filing should be started when the kitten is very young. Starting this when the cat has matured is much more difficult and may even be dangerous.

There are ways to control annoying cat scratching. Certainly, the easiest way is to present your cat with an acceptable cat scratching post. These are usually available at most local pet shops. The post should be covered with a material that is to your cat's liking. If your cat has already indicated what it likes to scratch, it usually is a good idea to cover the post with this same material. Veterinary surgeons often suggest that you use sandpaper, as this will reduce the cat's nails quickly and it will not have the urge to scratch. Certainly using hemp, carpeting, cotton towelling or bark is worth a try. Once the cat uses the post, it usually will have neither a desire nor a need to scratch any place else.

Besides the physical need to scratch, many cats have a psychological need to scratch. This is

CAT SCRATCH DISEASE

An objectionable habit of many poorly raised kittens is their exuberant jumping to greet you. This flying jump may result in the kitten's being attached to your body; otherwise it will fall to the floor and may injure itself. In the attachment process, your skin will usually be pierced, and this is a health concern. All cat scratches and bites should be thoroughly cleaned with an antiseptic soap. If a sore appears at the site of the wound, you should visit your family doctor immediately.

Cat scratch disease is a well-known problem. It is caused by a bacterium *(Rochalimaea henselae)* that is usually easily treated with antibiotics. However, more and more cases show resistance to the usual antibiotics.

Untreated cat scratch fever may result in an enlargement of the lymph nodes, imitating a cancerous condition known as lymphoma. Interestingly enough, the lymph nodes, upon biopsy, may show large Reid-Sternberg cells, which are a characteristic of Hodgkins lymphoma. The bottom line is that cat scratches should be taken seriously.

MAN MEETS CAT

Early man, perhaps 8000 years ago, started his symbiotic relationship with domestic cats, *Felis catus* or *Felis domesticus*. The cats killed and ate the rats and mice, and probably anything else which crawled and was small, which early man attracted and considered as pests. Early man reciprocated by allowing the cat to sleep in his cave, hut or tent. Cats, being essentially nocturnal, kept the small mammals (rats, mice, etc.) from disturbing the sleep of early man.

As early man matured to modern man, the domestic cat came along as an aid to pest control. This was especially true of peoples who farmed, as farmers were plagued with rodents. Though most cats were not selectively bred for their predatory skills, it was obvious that those cats that were the best hunters were more successful in evolutionary terms than the cats that were more meek. Modern cats have changed very little from the cats from which they descended. There are still, today, cats that are very predatory, attacking small mammals and birds; there are also meek cats which, unless fed by their owners, would perish in a competitive cat society.

It has been shown repeatedly that if kittens are socialised in a proper manner, they will become peaceful pets. This includes lions and tigers. If the kittens are not socialised properly, they revert immediately to their aggressive, predatory behaviours.

evidenced by where they scratch versus what they scratch. Often cats prefer semi-darkness. Some prefer flat surfaces and not vertical surfaces. Some prefer public areas in which their human friends are present instead of secluded areas. It may be stress related, as with scent marking, because scratching is another territorial-marking behaviour. In any case, the idea is to get your cat to scratch the post and not the carpets, furniture, drapes or the duvet on your bed.

Introduce your cat to the post by rubbing its paws on the post, hoping it will take the hint. Oftentimes the cat voluntarily attacks the post. Unfortunately, oftentimes it doesn't. If you catch your cat scratching in a forbidden area, startle it with a loud shout, by banging a folded newspaper against your hand or with something else which will take its attention away from scratching. Never hit the cat. This will only get a revengeful reaction that might be dangerous.

RUBBISH RUMMAGING

Cats are inquisitive and may decide to have a good look through any interesting rubbish bins that are exuding an enticing odour. Normally, the answer is to remove the bin. However, if the attraction always seems to be kitchen rubbish, there may be a nutritional problem. It may be searching for food because it is being underfed!

Introduce your Oriental to the scratching post by rubbing its paws on the post. Hopefully it will quickly catch on.

It may alternatively be receiving an unbalanced diet and is trying to satisfy its inner need for a given missing ingredient.

Another possibility, and one which may be more appropriate to the indoors-only cat, is boredom or loneliness. These conditions can only be remedied by greater interaction between owner and cat and/or obtaining a companion feline.

Clearly, the cause should be identified. The immediate solution is to place the rubbish in a cupboard or similar place that is out of the cat's reach. This type of solution is called removal of the re-enforcer. It is a common method of overcoming problems across a number of unwanted behaviours. However, it does not correct the underlying problem that must still be addressed.

The first-time cat owner should not think that the problems discussed will likely be encountered. They are only met when the cat's environment is lacking in some way. Always remember that the older cat may have problems with bowel control. An extra litter tray at another location in the home will usually remedy this situation. Finally, if a problem is found and you are not able to remedy it, do seek the advice of your vet or breeder.

While the idea of becoming a breeder may appeal to many owners, the reality is more difficult than is often appreciated. It requires dedication, considerable investment of time and money, and the ability to cope with many heart-wrenching decisions and failures.

It would be quite impossible to discuss the complexities of practical breeding in only one chapter, so we will consider the important requirements of being a breeder plus basic feline reproductive information. This will enable you to better determine if, indeed, this aspect of the hobby is for you.

BEING A BREEDER
Apart from great affection for the breed, a successful breeding programme requires quantifiable

> **FERAL CATS**
> Feral cats are, as a general rule, undernourished. They spend most of their time searching for food. Consequently, those feral cats that have kittens spend less time with their kittens than do well-nourished cats. It has been shown that kittens born to feral mothers are usually unsocial and show little affection for their mothers. Obviously, they would show a similar lack of affection for a human. That's one of the reasons that feral kittens make poor pets and should neither be adopted nor brought into your home. Kittens, which for any reason are separated from their mothers at the age of two weeks, develop an attitude of fear and wariness. They escape from contact with other cats or humans and can even be dangerous if they feel trapped.

objectives. Foremost among these is the rearing of healthy kittens free from known diseases. Next is the desire to produce offspring that are as good as, indeed better than, their parents.

Such objectives ensure that a breeder will endeavour to maintain standards and reduce or remove from the cat population

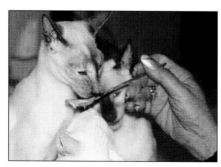

Raising a litter of kittens is only part of a breeder's many responsibilities.

any instances of dangerous diseases and conditions. Only stock registered and tested free of major diseases should ever be used. Adopting such a policy helps to counteract those who breed from inferior and often unhealthy cats.

To be a successful breeder, you will need to become involved in the competition side of the hobby. Only via this route will you be able to determine if your programme is successful or not. Always remember that even the top-winning breeders still produce quite a high percentage of kittens that will only be of pet quality. There will be many disappointments along the road to even modest success.

THE DISADVANTAGES OF BREEDING

There are many rewards to be gained from breeding, but the disadvantages should also be carefully considered. Kittens are

NEWBORN KITTENS

Most kittens are born with body hair. Their ears and eyes, however, remain closed for about two weeks, though some ears and eyes become functional after 72 hours. Kittens should be allowed to nurse for seven weeks, longer if they will not readily eat and drink from a plate. If allowed to nurse, most kittens will stay on their mother's milk for two months or more.

TIDY TOILETING

During the kitten's stay in the nest box, the mother will assist or even stimulate bowel and urine elimination, at least for the first month of the kitten's life. The mother also does the clean-up work in the nest box. But once the kitten is older, it becomes capable of relieving itself out of the nest box. Usually the kitten likes sand, soft earth or something that seems absorbent and is easily moved with its paws. By the time the kitten is two months old, it should develop the discipline of covering its elimination. Not all kittens develop this discipline, though the use of an absorbent clay litter seems to be helpful in developing this discipline in young cats. Your local pet shop will have various cat litters to offer you.

demanding, especially once they are over three weeks of age. Rearing, vaccination, registration and veterinary bills will be costly. Any thoughts of profit should be dispelled. Homes must be found for the kittens, which will entail receiving many telephone calls— some at very inconvenient hours.

Many potential buyers will prove to be either unsuitable or 'time-wasters' looking for the cheapest pedigreed cat obtainable. Kittens may die, while cats of any age could test positive for a major disease. They may have to be put to sleep or given to a caring person who understands the problem.

TOM FOOLERY

A non-neutered male cat kept as a single pet has little or no value for breeding purposes. It must be exhibited so it can gain some fame. The owner must have modern facilities to house both males and females. Females are always serviced at the home of the stud owner. This is extra responsibility and cost.

Such a male cannot be given any freedom to roam. If the tom is kept indoors, its scent-marking odours will often become intolerable. Even kept outdoors in a suitable cat pen, it will spray regularly to attract the attention of any females in the area. Toms are more assertive and often more aggressive than neutered males.

If they are allowed any outdoor freedom, they will become involved in battles with the local toms. Consequently, they will soon lose their handsome looks! Most cat breeders do not even keep males because of the problems and costs they entail. These cats are best kept in catteries where the owners have the time, the funds and everything else needed to justify their retention.

Owning a number of cats will mean investing in cat pens. When females come into heat, they will try to escape and mate with any local tom with a twinkle in his eye! Their scent and calls will attract roving Romeos who will gather near your home and involve themselves in a series of raucous battles. Holidays and matings will need to be planned around hoped-for litter dates. All in all, owning only one or two breeding females is a major commitment.

Before deciding whether breeding really is something you want to do, what would make good sense would be to neuter the pet and then become an exhibitor. When you have exhibited a number of times, your knowledge of cats will be greater, as will your contacts. You will be more aware of what quality is all about and what it will cost for a well-bred female. It will be like an apprenticeship. Whether you then become a breeder, remain an exhibitor or prefer life as a pet owner, you will be glad you heeded the words of advice given here.

STOCK SELECTION

Stock selection revolves around health, quality, sex and age. Before these are discussed, it should be stated that many beginners unwisely rush this process. It is essential that ample time be devoted to researching from whom to purchase. This decision will influence a novice breeder's entire future endeavours.

HEALTH

Cats should only be obtained from a breeder whose stock has

been tested negative for FeLV, FIP and FIV. The stock should be current on all vaccinations and worm treatments. Additionally, its blood type should be known so as to avoid incompatibility problems.

QUALITY

This must come in two forms. One is in the individual cat's appearance; the other is in its genetic ability to pass on the quality of its parents. The best way of obtaining these paired needs is to obtain initial stock from a breeder having a proven record of success in Oriental Shorthairs, and with the colour you plan to start with. Being well acquainted with the breed's standard will be advantageous when seeking foundation stock. A female show cat attains her titles based on her appearance, but she may not pass on those looks to her offspring. Another cat that is very sound may pass on most of her good points and thus be more valuable for breeding. Of course, all litters will be influenced by the quality of the tom used. He will account for 50% of the offspring's genes. When viewing a litter of kittens, never forget that they are the result of the genes of two cats.

SEX

The beginner should only obtain females. The best advice is to commence with just one very

TOO MANY CATS

There are already too many cats in the world. In many countries, thousands of pathetic-looking felines can be seen wandering the streets in a badly emaciated state. They live tormented lives and have become a major social problem in many areas. There can be no excuse for these feral populations in developed Western nations. Quite frankly, some people who own cats, including some pedigreed owners, lack a sense of responsibility.

Cats allowed to roam in a non-neutered state are by far the main reason for the overpopulation problem. Unless a cat is of show or breeding quality, there is not a single justification for it to be bred or to remain in a non-neutered state. If your cat was purchased as a pet, you should help to resolve this global problem by having it neutered at the earliest possible date. This will make it a far healthier, happier and less problematic pet.

When choosing breeding stock, never be dazzled by a pedigree. No matter how illustrious this is, it is only ever as good as the cat that bears it. If the cat is mediocre, then its prestigious pedigree is worthless from a breeding perspective. There are many other pitfalls for the novice when judging the value of a breeding line. These you must research in larger, more specialised books.

A lilac-coloured Oriental.

CAVEAT EMPTOR

When purchasing a kitten for breeding, make certain that the seller knows what your intentions are. If a kitten is registered on the non-active register, this means it was not considered by its breeder to be good enough for breeding. Any kittens bred from such a cat cannot be registered. You should also check that the mother of the kitten/young adult you are interested in has tested negative for feline leukaemia and that all other vaccinations are current.

time and money. A male is not needed until a breeder has become established. Even then, owning one is not essential to success. There is no shortage of quality

sound female. By the time you have exhibited her and gained more knowledge about the finer points of the breed, you will be far better able to judge what true quality is all about. By then, you will also have made many contacts on the show circuit. Alternatively, you may decide breeding is not for you and will have invested the minimum of

When purchasing an Oriental Shorthair kitten, health, soundness and personality are the buyer's primary considerations.

THE HEAT IS ON

Most female cats reach sexual maturity by the time they are 28 weeks old. Females normally accept males from late winter to early fall, about a six-month period. They have a reproductive cycle of about two weeks and are in heat for about one of the two weeks. Intercourse causes the female to ovulate and pregnancy may last for about 64 days, perhaps longer in cold climates and shorter in the tropics.

studs. Males create many problems the novice can do without. Once experience is gained is the time to decide if owning a male would be of any particular benefit.

AGE

There is no specific age at which stock should be purchased, but the following are suggested:

1. Most people purchase young kittens so they can enjoy them. However, with such youngsters, their ultimate quality is harder to assess.
2. Chances are improved if a kitten has already won awards in shows. This will be when she is 14 weeks to 9 months of age, but she will be more costly.
3. A quality young female that has already produced offspring is a prudent choice but will be the most expensive option.

THE BREEDING PROCESS

Sexual maturity in cats may come as early as four months of age.

ROAMING ROMEOS

Males cats, toms, have extended testicles very early in life. By about nine months of age, the tom is capable of mating with a queen. Both queens and toms are polygamous, and it is not uncommon for a queen to have a litter containing kittens fathered by different toms.

CAT CALLS

Females left in a non-spayed state are far more at risk from diseases and infections of the uterus. When in heat, the female becomes unusually affectionate and provocative. Her calls, a sound once heard never forgotten, can become extremely annoying if she is left unmated.

Breeding should not be considered until the female is at least 12 months old, especially in the slow-maturing breeds such as those of Persian and European stock ancestry. A young cat barely out of her kitten stage may not have the required physical or psychological stability to produce and raise a vigorous litter. After her first heat, a female will normally come into heat again every two to three weeks and continue to do so until mated. The actual oestrous period lasts three to eight days. It is during this time that she is receptive to a male.

Once the mating has been successful, the time between fertilisation and birth of the young, known as the gestation period, is in the range of 59 to 67 days, 63 or 64 days being typical. The litter size will generally be two to five. Kittens are born blind and helpless, but develop rapidly. Their eyes open at about the seventh day. By 21 days they

THE MALE STUD

The selection of a suitable stud should have been planned months before, as it can take some time to find the best male to use. It is preferred that the breeding lines of the stud are compatible with those of the female, meaning both pedigrees will carry a number of the same individuals in them. This is termed line-breeding. The ideal male will excel in those features that are considered weak in the female. You may read in other books that if a female is weak in a given feature, the ideal stud will be the total opposite. However, this can be misleading.

If the female has an overly long tail, what you do not need is a stud with a short tail. Rather, his tail should be as near the ideal length as possible. Genetically, this will improve tail length in your line without introducing unwanted genetic variance in your stock. Compensatory matings, such as short tail to long tail, will create such a variance. Once a male has been selected, ensure all his papers and vaccinations are in order. The female will be taken to the stud and left with him for a few days.

from your cat-registration authority. You should also consider the benefits of registering your own breeder prefix. This, however, is only worthwhile if you intend to breed on a more than casual basis. If you have decided that certain kittens are unsuitable for showing/breeding, do consider early neutering.

A well-bred Oriental Shorthair shimmers quality from every hair, as this dashing black silver shaded naturally conveys.

start exploring. At this time they will also be sampling solid foods. By eight weeks they can be vaccinated and neutered if required. Weaning normally commences by the age of six weeks and is completed within two to three weeks. Kittens can go to new homes when 12 weeks old, though 14 to 16 weeks is preferred.

During this period you must decide if you wish to register the kittens or merely 'declare' them. This allows them to be registered at a later time. Obtain the necessary information and forms

THE BREEDING QUEEN

A female used for breeding purposes is called a queen. The principal requirement of such a cat is that she is an excellent example of the breed. This does not mean she must be a show winner. Many a winning exhibition cat has proved to have little breeding value. This is because a show cat gains success purely on its appearance; however, it may not pass those looks to its offspring.

A good breeding female may lack that extra something needed to be a top winner. Yet, she may pass on most of her excellent features to her offspring. Much will depend on the breeding line from which she was produced. Therefore, any potential breeder must research existing breeders to ascertain which have good track records of producing consistently high-quality cats. In truth, and sadly, few newcomers in their haste to become breeders make this extra effort. This can result in becoming disillusioned if the female produces only average to inferior kittens.

Selecting an appealing kitten, of the colour of your choice, should be an exciting experience. Provided you have done your homework and have found a healthy litter, you have many joys ahead of you.

EXAMPLES OF CLASSES AT SHOWS

Open	Any cat of the specified breed.
Novice	Cats that have never won a first prize.
Limit	Cats that have not won more than first prizes.
Junior	Cats over nine months of age but less than two years on the day of the show.
Senior	Cats over two years old.
Visitors	Cats living a given distance away from the show venue.
Assessment	Experimental breeds, which have an approved standard.
Aristocrat	Cats with one or two Challenge Certificates (or Premiers for neuters) so are not yet full Champions/Premiers.

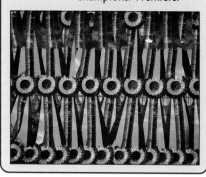

Without shows, the cat fancy could not exist. There would be only a handful of breeds as compared with today's ever-growing list. There would be fewer colour patterns and far less cat awareness. Given the great importance of shows to the cat fancy, it is perhaps a little surprising, and disappointing, that the majority of cat owners have never visited a feline exhibition.

Shows such as the National and the Supreme of Britain, or their equivalents in other countries, are the shop windows of the world of domestic cats. They are meeting places where breeders from all over the country compete to establish how well their breeding programmes are developing. A show is also a major social event on the cat calendar.

Whether a potential pet owner or breeder of the future, you should visit one or two shows. It is a great day out for the whole family. Apart from the wonderful selection of breeds, there are also many trade stands. If a product is available, it will be seen at the large exhibitions.

Many of the national clubs

and magazines have stands. The two major shows mentioned are held in the winter months, usually November and December. However, there are hundreds of other shows staged during the year in various parts of the country. They range from small local club events to major championship breed shows and are usually advertised in the cat magazines. Your ruling cat association can also supply a list of shows.

SHOW ORGANISATION

So you will have some idea of how things are organised, the following information will be helpful. You will learn even more by purchasing the show catalogue. This contains the names and addresses of the exhibitors and details of their cats. It also lists the prizes, indicates the show regulations and carries many interesting advertisements.

A major show revolves around three broad categories of cats:
1. Unaltered cats, meaning those that are capable of breeding.
2. Neuters.
3. Non-pedigreed cats.

There is, thus, the opportunity for every type of cat, from the best Oriental Shorthair to the everyday 'moggie' pets, to take part. These three broad categories are divided into

> ### CLASSES FOR NON-PEDIGREED CATS
> For non-pedigreed cats there are many classes, which include those for single colours, bicolours, tabbies, half-pedigreed, and so on. In this section are many delightful classes, such as those for cats owned by senior citizens, by young children (by age group), best original stray or rescued cat, best personality, most unusual looking, most photogenic and best older cats. Within this cat section can be seen some truly gorgeous felines. There is no doubt that the pet classes have been the springboard that has launched many a top breeder into the world of pedigreed cats.

various sections. For example, the unaltered and neuters are divided into their respective sections, such as Longhair, Semi-Longhair, British, Foreign, Siamese and so on.

There are many more classes other than those mentioned. These include club classes and those for kittens and non-pedigreed cats.

JUDGING

There are two ways that cats can be judged. One is pen judging, the other is bench or ring judging. In Britain, pen judging

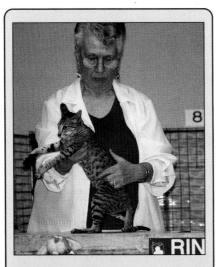

'VETTING IN'

In England, cats are examined by a veterinary surgeon upon arrival to a show to make sure that they appear healthy. This process is called 'vetting in.' If the cat is rejected, it can not be exhibited again until it receives a 'clearance certificate.' The reasons for rejection are stated in the rule book, which can be obtained at the show.

then competes against other breed winners for the Best in Group award. The group winners compete for the Best in Show award.

ON THE CONTINENT AND BEYOND...

In Britain, the title of UK Grand Champion or Premier is won in competition with other Grand titleholders. In mainland Europe, cats can become International Champions. More British cats are expected to become International Champions with the recent introduction of passports for cats, allowing cats to compete more freely on the Continent and beyond. In countries other than Britain, the way in which shows are organised and titles achieved do differ somewhat. However, they broadly follow the outline discussed here.

is the normal method, though bench judging is used for Best in Show. In pen judging, the judge moves around the cat pens. The cat gaining the most points when compared to the standard wins. In bench judging, stewards take the cats to the judge.

If a cat wins its class, it then competes against other class winners. By this process of elimination, a cat may go on to win the Best of Breed award. It

This lovely lilac Oriental Shorthair enjoys a successful show career.

A breeder can gather a number of awards during the course of a show. Even those who do not own the very best cats can take pride in gaining second, third, fourth and recommended, especially if won at the larger shows. By progression, the top cat at a show will win its class, its breed, its section, and ultimately become the Best in Show exhibit. The titles a cat can win commence with that of Champion, or Premier in the case of neuters. A Grand Champion is made after winning in competition with others of its same status. The same applies to a Grand Premier. The judging system may vary from one country to another, but the basis remains as outlined.

THE SHOW CAT

When a cat is seen preening in its pen, the hard work that has gone into its preparation is rarely appreciated. Exhibits must be in peak condition and their coats in full bloom. The potential exhibit must be gradually trained to spend hours in its show pen. It must display no fear or aggression towards strangers, such as the stewards or the judges. These must be able to physically

BECOMING AN EXHIBITOR

Before any hobbyist enters a show, he is advised to join a local cat club. Here, hobbyists will meet local breeders who will not only assess their cats for them but also provide help on many other topics. The novice exhibitor could attend one or two shows with an exhibitor in order to learn the ropes. During this period, he can become familiar with the show rules and regulations. These are quite extensive, intended to safeguard the best interests of the hobby, the exhibitors and, most importantly, the cats.

It is of interest to note that some breeders own cats in partnership with other fanciers. This is useful when one person enjoys the breeding and the other the exhibition side. It enables both to really be involved in the hobby to a level that might not have been possible for either on his own. So, whether you fancy being an exhibitor or just love cats, do make a point of visiting the next major show in your area. You may just find the experience rewarding.

Apart from being comfortable with people peering into its pen, the cat must be able to endure long journeys to the show venue. Unless properly trained, the cat may become a nervous, aggressive feline that will have a very short show career.

Obviously the cat must display quality. This means having none of the major faults that would prevent it from gaining a first prize. These are listed in the breed standard. The meaning of quality is very flexible. You do not need to own a potential champion to be a successful exhibitor. The cat must also be registered with the association under whose rules the show is being run. In Britain, this will be the Governing Council of the Cat Fancy (GCCF) or The Cat Association of Britain.

As in anything competitive, exhibits can gain prizes at the lower levels of a hobby without having any realistic chance of awards in the major shows. Owning such exhibits is often part of a top breeder/exhibitor's portfolio from their early days in the hobby. Others may never move beyond the smaller shows but still gain reputations for owning sound stock. They thoroughly enjoy being involved at their given level.

If the idea of exhibiting appeals to you, the best way to make a start is to join a local

examine it, including its ears and teeth; it also involves being lifted into the air. If a cat scratches or bites a judge, or any other show official, it is automatically withdrawn from the show. A repeat of this in the future would result, in most instances, in the cat's show career being terminated by the ruling association.

club. There you will not only be advised on all procedures, but will assuredly make many new friends. Exhibiting can be costly in cash and time, but you can focus on the more local shows while attending the larger ones as a visitor.

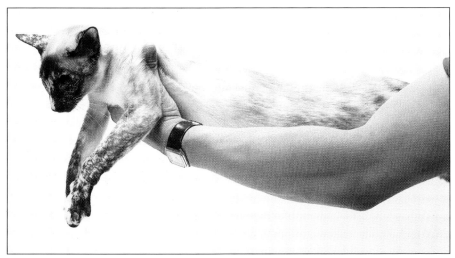

A show cat must tolerate all types of handling during the judging sessions. A cat that bites or scratches is usually eliminated from the show.

A cock-of-the-walk Black Oriental Shorthair, showing off his confident stature and impressive tail.

Maintaining a cat in the peak of good health revolves around the implementation of a sound husbandry strategy. At the basic level, this means being responsible about feeding, cleanliness and grooming. However, in spite of an owner's best efforts in these matters, cats may still become ill due to other causes. Although owners can attempt to prevent, identify and react to problems, only a vet is qualified to diagnose and advise and/or effect remedies. Attempts by owners or 'informed' friends to diagnose and treat for specific diseases are dangerous and potentially life-threatening to the cat.

A LONG, HEALTHY LIFE

As veterinary surgeons make medical advances in the health care of cats, the longevity of the typical house cat is improving. Certainly ages between 15 and 18 years are not uncommon, and reports of cats living more than 20 years are predictable.

SELECTING A VETERINARY SURGEON

Your selection of a veterinary surgeon should not be based upon personality (as most are) but upon convenience to your home. You want a vet who is close because you might have emergencies or need to make multiple visits for treatments. You want a vet who has services that you might require such as nail clipping and bathing, as well as sophisticated pet supplies and a good reputation for ability and responsiveness. There is nothing more frustrating than having to wait a day or more to get a response from your veterinary surgeon.

All veterinary surgeons are licensed and their diplomas and/or certificates should be

displayed in their waiting rooms. There are, however, many veterinary specialities that usually require further studies and internships. There are specialists in heart problems (veterinary cardiologists), skin problems (veterinary dermatologists), teeth and gum problems (veterinary dentists), eye problems (veterinary ophthalmologists) and x-rays (veterinary radiologists), as well as vets who have specialities in reproduction, nutrition and behaviour. Most veterinary surgeons do routine surgery, such as neutering and stitching up wounds. When the problem affecting your cat is serious, it is not unusual or impudent to get another medical opinion, although in Britain you are obliged to advise the vets concerned about this. You might also want to compare costs among several veterinary surgeons. Sophisticated health care and veterinary services can be very costly. It is not infrequent that important decisions are based upon financial considerations.

PREVENTATIVE MEDICINE

It is much easier, less costly and more effective to practise preventative medicine than to fight bouts of illness and disease. Properly bred kittens come from parents who were selected based upon their genetic disease profile. Their mothers should have been

KEEPING YOUR CAT HEALTHY

Although there are a multitude of ailments, diseases and accidents that could befall a cat, all but the most minor of problems can be avoided with good management. The following tips are a recipe for keeping your cat in the peak of health.

- Make sure it is vaccinated and in other ways protected from each of the major diseases. It must also receive annual boosters to maintain immunity.
- Have periodic checks made by your vet to see if your cat has worms.
- Ensure the cat receives an adequate diet that is both appealing and balanced.
- Have the kitten neutered if it is not to be used for breeding.
- Ensure the cat's litter tray, food/water vessels and grooming tools are always maintained in spotless condition.
- Do not let your cat out overnight or when you are away working or shopping.
- Always wash your hands after gardening or petting other people's pets.
- Groom your cat daily. If this is done, you will more readily notice fleas or other problems than if grooming was done less frequently.
- Never try to diagnose and treat problems that are clearly of an internal type. Remember, even the most informed of breeders is not a vet and unable to reliably diagnose problems for you or suggest treatments. Contact your vet.
- If you are ever in doubt about the health of your cat, do not delay in discussing your concerns with your vet. Delays merely allow problems to become more established.

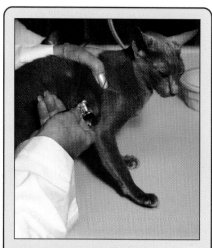

A DELICATE HEART

A cat's heart is as delicate as a human's heart, but it is much smaller. At full maturity, a queen's heart weighs between 9–12 grammes. A tom's heart is heavier, weighing 11–18 grammes. The blood that circulates through the heart chambers does not supply the heart muscle, thus requiring a separate circulatory system for the heart muscle.

VACCINATIONS

Most vaccinations are given by injection and should only be done by a veterinary surgeon. Both he and you should keep a record of the date of the injection, the identification of the vaccine and the amount given. The first vaccination is normally given when the kitten is about 8–9 weeks old. About 30 days later, a booster is given. Although

THE RIB CAGE

Cats usually have 13 pairs of ribs. The ribs in the middle are longer than the ribs on either end (or beginning) of the rib cage. The first nine ribs are joined to the chest bone (sternum) with costal cartilages. Ribs 10, 11 and 12 are also associated with cartilage, which contributes to the costal arch. The thirteenth rib is called the floating rib and its cartilage is separate from the other ribs.

vaccinated, free of all internal and external parasites and properly nourished. For these reasons, a visit to the veterinary surgeon who cared for the queen is recommended. The queen passes on disease resistance to her kittens, which can last for eight to ten weeks. She can also pass on parasites and many infections. That's why you should visit the veterinary surgeon who cared for the queen.

BLOOD GROUP INCOMPATIBILITY (BGI)

In recent years blood group incompatibility has become the focus of scientists, vets and breeders. Its importance to pet owners is when transfusions are needed. For breeders it probably accounts for a large percentage of kittens that die from fading kitten syndrome. Scientifically the problem is called neonatal erythrolysis, meaning the destruction of red blood cells in newly born offspring.

Cats have two blood groups, A & B. Group A is dominant to B (which is genetically called recessive). When the antibodies of B-group mothers are passed to A-group kittens, via her colostrum milk, they destroy red blood cells. Death normally follows within a few days.

Most domestic cats tested are group A. However, national and regional differences display a variation in which 1-6% may be of type B. In pedigreed breeds it has been found that the number of group-B cats varies significantly. The following breeds, based on present available data, have the indicated percentage incidence of group-B blood type.

0%	Siamese, Burmese and Oriental Shorthair
1-5%	Maine Coon, Manx and Norwegian Forest
10-20%	Abyssinian, Birman, Japanese Bobtail, Persian, Scottish Fold and Somali
25-50%	British Shorthair, Devon and Cornish Rex and Exotic Shorthair

The clear implication to breeders is to establish their cats' blood group, via testing, and conduct appropriate matings. These should not result in B-group mothers nursing A-group kittens.

The safe matings are:

1. Group-A males   x A females
2. Group-B males   x A or B females
3. Group-A females x A or B males
4. Group-B females x B males

Breeders are advised to seek further information before embarking on stock purchase and breeding programmes.

there are many diseases to which a cat may fall victim, the most dangerous three—FIE, FVR and FeLV—can be safeguarded against with a single (three-in-one) injection. Thereafter, an annual booster is all that is required.

MAJOR DISEASES

There are a number of diseases for which there is either no cure or little chance of recovery. However, some can be prevented by vaccination. All breeders and owners should ensure kittens are so protected.

FELINE INFECTIOUS ENTERITIS (FIE)

This is also known as feline panleukopenia, feline distemper and feline parvovirus. The virus

CLEANLINESS IS THE KEY

Crucial to the prevention and spread of disease is the need to maintain meticulous cleanliness, especially relating to the litter tray. Many diseases and problems are transferred via faecal matter. Once a problem is suspected, the advice of a vet should be sought. Blood tests, faecal microscopy and other testing methods are now available. They can make the difference between life and death for a cherished pet.

attacks the intestinal system. It is spread via the faeces and urine. The virus may survive for many years in some environments. The use of household bleach (sodium

HEALTH AND VACCINATION SCHEDULE

AGE	6 WKS	8 WKS	10 WKS	12 WKS	16 WKS	6 MOS	1 YR
Worm control	✔	✔	✔		✔		
Neutering						✔	
Rhinotracheitis	✔	✔		✔	✔		✔
Panleukopenia	✔	✔		✔			✔
Calcivirus		✔			✔		✔
Feline Leukaemia				✔			✔
Feline Infectious Peritonitis				✔	✔		✔
Faecal evaluation						✔	
Feline Immunodeficiency testing							✔
Feline Leukaemia testing				✔			✔
Dental evaluation		✔				✔	
Rabies				✔	✔		✔

Vaccinations are not instantly effective. It takes about two weeks for the cat's immune system to develop antibodies. Most vaccinations require annual booster shots. Your veterinary surgeon should guide you in this regard.

DISEASE REFERENCE CHART

	What is it?	Cause	Symptoms
Feline Leukaemia Virus (FeLV)	Infectious disease; kills more cats each year than any other feline infectious disease.	A virus spread through saliva, tears, urine and faeces of infected cats; bite wounds.	Early on no symptoms may occur, but eventually infected cats experience signs from depression and weight loss to respiratory distress. FeLV also suppresses immune system, making a cat susceptible to almost any severe chronic illness.
Rabies	Potentially deadly virus that infects warm-blooded mammals. Not seen in the United Kingdom.	A bacterium, which is often carried by rodents, that enters through mucous membranes and spreads quickly throughout the body.	Aggressiveness, a blank or vacant look in the eyes, increased vocalisation and/or weak or wobbly gait.
Feline Infectious Enteritis (FIE) *aka Panleukopenia*	Highly contagious virus, potentially deadly.	Ingestion of the virus, which is usually spread through the faeces of infected cats.	Most common: severe diarrhoea. Also vomiting, fatigue, lack of appetite, severe inflammation of intestines.
Feline Viral Rhinotracheitis (FVR)	Viral disease that affects eyes and upper respiratory tracts.	A virus that can affect any cat, especially those in multiple-cat settings.	Sneezing attacks, coughing, drooling thick saliva, fever, watery eyes, ulcers of mouth, nose and eyes.
Feline Immuno-deficiency Virus (FIV)	Virus that reduces white blood cells.	An infection spread commonly through cat-fight wounds.	Signs may be dormant for years or innocuous, such as diarrhoea or anaemia.
Feline Infectious Peritonitis (FIP)	A fatal viral disease, may be linked to FeLV and FIV.	Bacteria in dirty litter boxes; stress may increase susceptibility in kittens.	Extremely variable; range from abdominal swelling to chest problems, eye ailments and body lesions.
Feline Urological Syndrome (FUS)	A disease that affects the urinary tracts of cats.	Inflammation of bladder and urethra.	Constipation, constant licking of penis or vulva, blood in urine (males), swollen abdomen, crying when lifted.

hypochlorite) for cleaning helps to prevent colonisation. Signs, among others, are diarrhoea, vomiting, depression, anorexia and dehydration. Death may occur within days. A vaccine is available.

CARE OF THE FELINE KIDNEYS
The kidney of the cat is larger than that of the dog, but it has the typical bean shape. It receives 25% of the blood output of the heart! For this reason, it has rather significant veins to accommodate this large supply of blood, and injuries suffered by the kidneys are usually serious and not uncommon.

FELINE VIRAL RHINOTRACHEITIS (FVR) & CALCIVIRUS (FCV)
Also known as cat flu, this is a complex of upper respiratory diseases. Signs are excessive hard sneezing, runny nose and mouth ulcers. Cats vaccinated after having contracted flu may recover but may suffer recurrent bouts, especially if they become stressed.

NEUTERING

Neutering is a major means of avoiding ill health. It dramatically reduces the risk of males' becoming involved in territorial battles with the dangers of physical injury and disease transference. It makes the male more placid and less likely to scent mark its home. It also reduces the incidence of prostate problems and there is no risk of testicular cancer. The female avoids potentially lethal illnesses related to her being allowed to remain in an unmated condition, such as breast cancer.

Neutering is usually performed between six and four months of age, but it can be done as early as eight weeks of age. Data available on the age at which a kitten is neutered indicate that early neutering has more advantages than drawbacks. Breeders should have this performed on all cats sold as pets.

Male cats are neutered. The operation removes the testicles and requires that the cat be anaesthetised. Females are spayed. This is a major surgery during which the ovaries and uterus are removed. Both males and females should be kept quiet at home for about seven to ten days following the procedure, at which time the vet will remove the sutures.

A show-quality cinnamon-coloured Oriental Shorthair.

FELINE LEUKAEMIA VIRUS (FeLV)

This is a highly infectious viral disease. It is spread via direct contact—mutual grooming, saliva, feeding bowls, faeces, urine and biting. It can be passed prenatally from a female to her offspring. It creates tumours, anaemia, immune system depression, pyrexia (high temperatures), lethargy, respiratory disease, intestinal disease and many other potentially fatal problems. It is most prevalent in high-density cat populations. Not all cats will be affected, but they may become carriers.

Kittens less than six months old are especially vulnerable. Infected cats usually die by the time they are three to four years old. Cats can be screened or tested for this disease. Vaccination is not 100% effective but is recommended in kittens being sold into multi-cat environments.

FELINE IMMUNODEFICIENCY VIRUS (FIV)

This causes the white blood cells to be significantly reduced, thus greatly suppressing the efficiency of the immune system. It is not transferable to humans. Infection is normally gained from cat-fight wounds; thus, outdoor males are at the most risk. A cat diagnosed via blood tests as FIV-positive may live a normal life for months or years if retained indoors and given careful attention. Signs may

HEALTHY CAT

The enormous population of pet cats has stimulated the veterinary medical community to learn more about cats and to develop more modern medicines to keep felines healthier.

be innocuous in the early stages, such as anaemia or diarrhoea. No vaccine is available.

FELINE INFECTIOUS PERITONITIS (FIP)

This viral disease is invariably fatal once contracted in its more potent forms. However, the virulence of the virus is variable and may by destroyed by the immune system. Stress may increase susceptibility in kittens. It may be linked to FeLV and FIV. Signs are extremely variable and range from abdominal swelling to chest problems, eye ailments to body lesions. There are various tests available, but none is as yet 100% conclusive. Strict cleanliness is essential, especially of litter trays. No vaccine is available.

FELINE UROLOGICAL SYNDROME (FUS)

This is a very distressing condition caused by an inflammation of the bladder and urethra. Signs are constipation-like squatting and attempts to urinate, regular licking of the penis or vulva, blood in urine (males), swollen abdomen, crying

when lifted and urinating in unusual places (often only small amounts).

The numerous causes include: infection, dirty litter tray of the indoor cat, alkaline urine (in cats it should be acidic), diet too dry, lack of water intake (even though this may be available) and being hit by a vehicle (damaged nerves). Veterinary treatment is essential or the condition could be fatal due to bladder bursting or presence of dangerous bacteria.

Cream-coloured Oriental Shorthair.

Vaccinations are a must for all pet cats and dogs. They not only protect your pet...they also protect you.

STRESS TEST

Stress reduces the effectiveness of the immune system. Seemingly innocuous conditions may develop into major problems or leave the cat more open to attack by disease. Stress is difficult to specifically identify, but its major causes are well known. These include incorrect diet, intrusion by another cat in its home or territory, excessive handling and petting, disturbed sleep, uncomfortable home temperatures, bullying by another cat or pet, parasitic infestation, boarding in a cattery, travel, moving, boredom, limited accommodation space and, for some felines, being exhibited.

RABIES

Britain and most European Community countries are free of this terrible disease. The stringent quarantine laws of Britain are such that vaccination is not necessary. However, the introduction of passports for dogs and cats means that resident British cats must be vaccinated if they are to travel abroad and return to the UK without being placed into quarantine. The vaccination is given when the kitten is three or more months old. The pet passport process takes at least six months to complete, so plan well ahead.

COMMON HEALTH PROBLEMS

DERMATITIS (ECZEMA)

Dry lifeless coat, loss of coat, tiny scabs over the head and body, loose flakes (dandruff) and excessive scratching are all commonly called eczema. The cause covers a range of possibilities including diet, parasitic mites such as *Cheyletiella spp*, fungus or an allergy to flea or other bites. Sometimes reasons are unknown. Veterinary diagnosis and treatment are required.

RINGWORM (*DERMATOPHYTOSIS*)

This problem is fungal, not that of a worm. The most common form is *Microsporum canis*, which accounts for over 90% of cases. Cats less than one year old are at the highest risk, while longhaired breeds are more prone to the problem than shorthaired cats. The fungi feed on the keratin layers of the skin, nails and hair. Direct contact and spores that remain in the environment are the main means of transmission.

Typical signs are circular-type

bald areas of skin, which may be flaked and reddish. The coat generally may become dry and lifeless, giving the appearance of numerous other skin and hair problems. Veterinary diagnosis and treatment, either topical or via drugs, is essential as the condition is zoonotic, meaning it can be transferred to humans.

EAR PROBLEMS

Most of the common ear problems affect the outer ear. The cat's constant scratching of the ears, holding the ear to one side, greasy hairs around the ear, dark brown wax (cerumen) in the ears, scaly flakes in or around the ear and minute white or orange pinhead-like bodies (mites) in the ear are common signs. Canker is a term used for ear infections, but it has no specific meaning.

Over-the-counter remedies for ear problems are ineffective unless correct diagnosis has been made. It is therefore better to let the vet diagnose and treat the cat. Some problems may require anaesthesia and minor surgery.

DIARRHOEA

This is a general term used to indicate a semi-liquid to liquid state of faecal matter. Mild to acute cases may be due to a change of home, dietary change, eating an 'off' item, gorging on a favoured food, stress or a minor chill. These often rectify

themselves within days. Chronic and persistent diarrhoea may be the result of specific diseases. Any indication of blood in the faecal matter must be

POSSIBLE SOURCES OF EAR PROBLEMS

- Fight scratches
- Excess secretion of wax
- Swellings and blood blisters (haematoma) resulting from intrusion by foreign bodies (grass, etc.)
- Sunburn
- Whitish-coloured ear mites (*Otodectes cynotis*)
- Orange-coloured harvest mites (*Trombicula autumnalis*)
- Fleas
- Bacterial infection of either the outer or middle/inner ear

considered dangerous.

In minor cases, withholding food for 12–24 hours, or feeding a simple diet, may arrest the condition. If not, wisdom suggests contacting your vet. Faecal analysis and blood testing may be required. By answering numerous questions related to the cat's diet, general health, level of activity, loss of appetite, etc., the vet will determine whether tests are required or if immediate treatment seems more appropriate. Do not give cats human or canine intestinal remedies; these could prove dangerous.

Red silver-shaded Oriental Shorthair.

CONSTIPATION

Constipation—when a cat strains but is unable to pass motions—can have many causes. The cat may have hairballs, may have eaten a bird or rodent and has a bone lodged in its intestinal tract, may be suffering from a urological problem rather than constipation, or may have been hit by a car and has damaged the nerves that control bowel movements. As constipation is potentially serious, veterinary advice should be sought. Laxatives and faecal-softener tablets may be given, the faecal matter can be surgically removed or other treatment carried out.

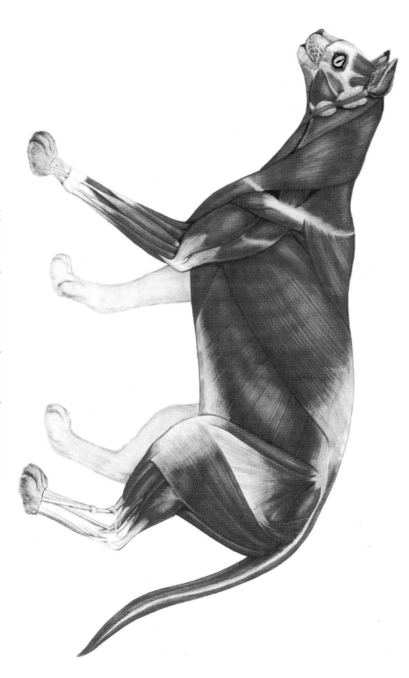

The cat's agile, athletic body is composed of a complex muscular system that a llows the feline unique flexibility.

*From the *Atlas of Feline Anatomy for Veterinarians* by Hudson/Hamilton. Published by W B Saunders Company.

EXTERNAL PARASITES

FLEAS

Of all the problems to which cats are prone, none is more well known and frustrating than fleas. Indeed, flea-related problems are the principal cause of visits to veterinary surgeons. Flea infestation is relatively simple to cure but difficult to prevent. Periodic flea checks for your cat, conducted as well as annual health check-ups, are highly recommended. Consistent dosing with anthelmintic preparations is also advised. Parasites that are harboured inside the body are a

bit more difficult to eradicate, but they are easier to control.

To control a flea infestation, you have to understand the flea's life cycle. Fleas are often thought of as a summertime problem but centrally heated homes have changed the life-cycle patterns, and fleas can be found at any time of the year. Fleas thrive in hot and humid environments; they soon die if the temperature drops below 35°F. The most effective method of flea control is a two-stage approach: one stage to kill the adult fleas, and the other to control the development of pre-adult fleas. Unfortunately, no

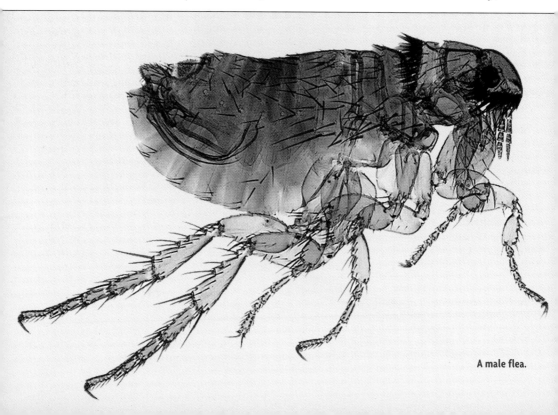

A male flea.

single active ingredient is effective against all stages of the life cycle.

LIFE CYCLE STAGES

During its life, a flea will pass through four life stages: egg, larva, pupa and adult. The adult stage is the most visible and irritating stage of the flea life cycle, and this is why the majority of flea-control products concentrate on this stage. The fact is that adult fleas account for only 1% of the total flea population, and the other 99% exist in pre-adult stages, i.e. eggs, larvae and pupae. The pre-adult stages are barely visible to the naked eye.

THE LIFE CYCLE OF THE FLEA

Eggs are laid on the cat, usually in quantities of about 20 or 30, several times a day. The female adult flea must have a blood meal before each egg-laying session. When first laid, the eggs will not cling to the cat's fur, as the eggs are not sticky. They will immediately fall to the floor or ground, especially if the cat moves around or scratches.

Once the eggs fall from the cat onto the carpet or furniture, they will hatch into yellow larvae, approximately 2 mms long. This takes from 5 to 11 days. Larvae are not particularly mobile and will

A Look at Fleas

Fleas have been around for millions of years and have adapted to changing host animals. They are able to go through a complete life cycle in less than one month, or they can extend their lives to almost two years by remaining as pupae or cocoons. They must have a blood meal every 10-14 days, and egg production begins within 2 days of their first meal. The female cat flea is very prolific and can lay 2000 eggs in her lifetime!

Fleas have been measured as being able to jump 300,000 times and can jump 150 times their body length in any direction, including straight up. Those are just a few of the reasons why they are so successful in infesting a cat!

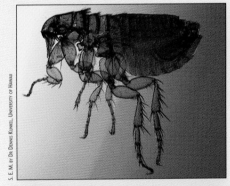

A scanning electron micrograph (S. E. M.) of a flea.

S. E. M. BY DR DENNIS KUNKEL, UNIVERSITY OF HAWAII

Magnified head of a flea.

S. E. M. BY DR DENNIS KUNKEL, UNIVERSITY OF HAWAII

usually travel only a few inches from where they hatch. However, they do have a tendency to move away from light and heavy traffic—under furniture, in the carpet and behind doors are common places to find high quantities of flea larvae.

The flea larvae feed on dead organic matter, including adult flea faeces, until they are ready to change into adult fleas. Fleas will usually remain as larvae for around seven days, becoming darker in colour. After this period, the larvae will pupate a protective cocoon. While inside the pupae, the larvae will undergo metamorphosis and change into adult fleas. This can happen within a week, but the adult fleas can remain inside the pupae waiting to hatch for up to six months. The pupae are signalled to hatch by certain stimuli, such as physical pressure—the pupae's being stepped on, heat from an animal lying on the pupae or increased carbon dioxide levels and vibrations—indicating that a suitable host is available.

DID YOU KNOW?
Never mix flea-control products without first consulting your veterinary surgeon. Some products can become toxic when combined with others and can cause serious or fatal consequences.

DID YOU KNOW?
Flea-killers are poisonous. You should not spray these toxic chemicals on areas of a cat's body that he licks, on his genitals or on his face. Flea killers taken internally are a better answer, but check with your vet in case internal therapy is not advised for your cat.

Once hatched, the adult flea must feed within a few days. Once the adult flea finds a host, it will not leave voluntarily. It only becomes dislodged by grooming or the host animal's scratching. The adult flea will remain on the host for the duration of its life unless forcibly removed.

TREATING THE ENVIRONMENT AND THE CAT
Treating fleas should be a two-pronged attack. First, the environment needs to be treated; this includes carpets and furniture, especially the cat's bedding and areas underneath furniture. The environment should be treated with a household spray containing an Insect Growth Regulator (IGR) and an insecticide to kill the adult fleas. There are also liquids, given orally, that contain chitin inhibitors. These render flea eggs incapable of development. There are both foam and liquid wipe-on treatments. Additionally, cats can

Opposite page: A scanning electron micrograph of a flea, magnified more than 100x. This image has been colorized for effect.

The Life Cycle of the Flea

Eggs

Larvae

Pupa

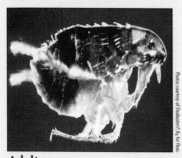

Adult

Photos courtesy of fleabusters®: Rx for fleas.

Flea Control

IGR (INSECT GROWTH REGULATOR)

Two types of products should be used when treating fleas—a product to treat the pet and a product to treat the home. Adult fleas represent 1% of the flea population. The pre-adult fleas (eggs, larvae and pupae) represent 99% of the flea population and are found in the environment; it is in the case of pre-adult fleas that products containing an Insect Growth Regulator (IGR) should be used in the home.

IGRs are a new class of compounds used to prevent the development of insects. They do not kill the insect outright, but instead use the insect's biology against it to stop it from completing its growth. Products that contain methoprene are the world's first and leading IGRs. Used to control fleas and other insects, this type of IGR will stop flea larvae from developing and protect the house for up to seven months.

EN GARDE:
CATCHING FLEAS OFF GUARD!

Consider the following ways to arm yourself against fleas:
• Add a small amount of pennyroyal or eucalyptus oil to your cat's bath. These natural remedies repel fleas.
• Supplement your cat's food with fresh garlic (minced or grated) and a hearty amount of brewer's yeast, both of which ward off fleas.
• Use a flea comb on your cat daily. Submerge fleas in a cup of bleach to kill them quickly.
• Confine the cat to only a few rooms to limit the spread of fleas in the home.
• Vacuum daily...and get all of the crevices! Dispose of the bag every few days until the problem is under control.
• Wash your cat's bedding daily. Cover cushions where your cat sleeps with towels, and wash the towels often.

be injected with treatments that can last up to six months. Emulsions that have the same effect can also be added to food. The advanced treatments are only available from veterinary surgeons. The IGRs actually mimic the fleas' own hormones and stop the eggs and larvae from developing into adult fleas. There are currently no treatments available to attack the pupa stage of the life cycle, so the adult insecticide is used to kill the newly hatched adult fleas before they find a host. Most IGRs are active for many months, while adult insecticides are only active for a few days.

When treating with a household spray, it is a good idea to vacuum before applying the product. This stimulates as many pupae as possible to hatch into adult fleas. The vacuum cleaner should also be treated with a flea treatment to prevent the eggs and larvae that have been hoovered into the vacuum bag from hatching.

The second stage of treatment is to apply an adult insecticide to the cat, usually in the form of a collar or a spray. Alternatively, there are drops that, when placed on the back of the animal's neck, spread throughout the fur and skin to kill adult fleas. A word of warning: Never use products sold for dogs on your cat; the result could be fatal.

PHOTO BY DWIGHT R KUHN

Dwight R Kuhn's magnificent action photo, showing a flea jumping.

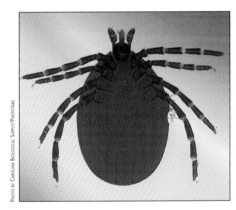

PHOTO BY CAROLINA BIOLOGICAL SUPPLY/PHOTOTAKE

A brown tick, *Rhipicephalus sanguineus*, is an uncommon but annoying tick found on cats.

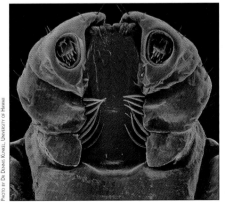

PHOTO BY DR DENNIS KUNKEL, UNIVERSITY OF HAWAII

The head of a tick, *Dermacentor variabilis*, enlarged and coloured for effect.

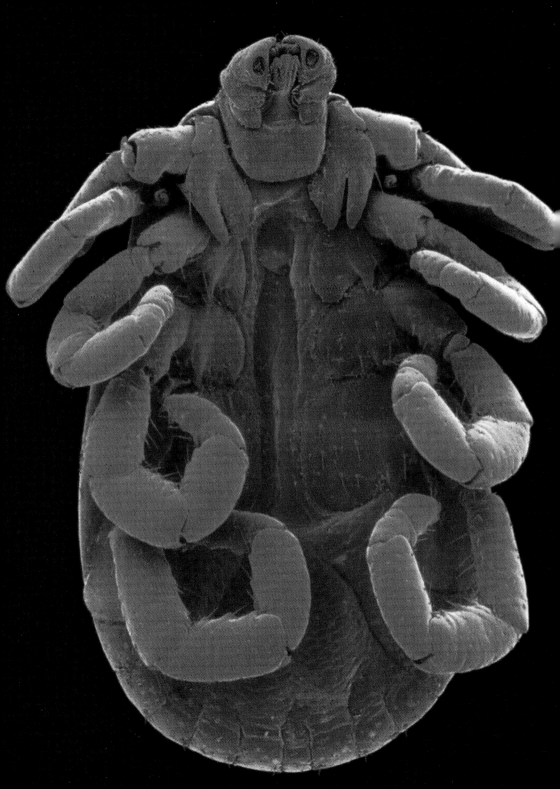

TICKS AND MITES

Though not as common as fleas, ticks and mites are found all over the tropical and temperate world. They don't bite, like fleas; they harpoon. They dig their sharp proboscis (nose) into the cat's skin and drink the blood. Their only food and drink is your cat's blood. Cats can get potentially fatal anaemia, paralysis and many other diseases from ticks and mites. They may live where fleas are found and they like to hide in cracks or seams in walls wherever cats live. They are controlled the same way fleas are controlled.

The *Dermacentor variabilis* may well be the most common tick in many geographical areas, especially those areas where the climate is hot and humid. The other common ticks that attack small animals are *Rhipicephalus sanguineus*, *Ixodes* and some species of *Amblyomma*.

Most ticks have life expectancies of a week to six months, depending upon climatic conditions. They can neither jump nor fly, but they can crawl slowly and can range up to 5 metres (16 feet) to reach a sleeping or unsuspecting animal.

INTERNAL PARASITES

Most animals—fishes, birds and mammals, including cats and humans—have worms and other parasites that live inside their bodies. According to Dr Herbert R Axelrod, the fish pathologist, there are two kinds of parasites: dumb and smart. The smart parasites live in peaceful cooperation with their hosts (symbiosis), while the dumb parasites kill their host. Most of the worm infections are relatively

---

TOXOPLASMOSIS AND PREGNANT WOMEN

Toxoplasmosis is caused by a single parasite, *Toxoplasma gondii*. Cats acquire it by eating infected prey, such as rodents or birds, or raw meat. Obviously, strictly indoor cats are at less risk of infection than cats that are permitted to roam outdoors. Symptoms include diarrhoea, listlessness, pneumonia and inflammation of the eye. Sometimes there are no symptoms. The disease can be treated with antibiotics.

The only way humans can get the disease is through direct contact with the cat's faeces. People usually don't display any symptoms, although they can show mild flu-like symptoms. Once exposed, an antibody is produced and the person builds immunity to the disease.

The real danger to humans is that pregnant women can pass the parasite to the developing foetus. In this case the chances are good that the baby will be born with a major health problem and/or serious birth defects. In order to eliminate risk, pregnant women should have someone else deal with the litter-box duties or wear gloves while taking care of the litter box and wash hands thoroughly afterwards.

Opposite page: The tick, *Dermacentor variabilis*, is one of the most common ticks found on cats. Look at the strength in its eight legs! No wonder it's hard to detach them.

INTERNAL PARASITES OF CATS

NAME	DESCRIPTION	SYMPTOMS	ACQUISITION	TREATMENT
Roundworm (*Toxocara cati* and *Toxascaris leonina*)	Large, white, coil-like worms, 2–4 inches long, resembling small springs.	Vomiting, pot belly, respiratory problems, poor growth rate, protruding third eyelids, poor haircoat.	Ingesting infective larvae; ingesting infected mammals, birds or insects; a queen with *Toxocari cati* nursing kittens.	Anthelmintics; scrupulously clean environment (e.g. daily removal of all faeces recommended).
***Physaloptera* species**	1–6 inches long, attacks the wall of the stomach.	Vomiting, anorexia, melena.	Eating insects that live in soil (e.g. May beetles).	Diagnosed with a gastroscope; treated with pyrantel pamoate. Prevention of exposure to the intermediate hosts.
***Gordius* or Horsehair worm**	6-inch pale brown worms with stripes.	Vomiting.	May ingest a worm while drinking from or making contact with swimming pools and toilet bowls.	Anthelmintics; avoiding potentially infected environments.
Hookworm (*Ancylostoma tubaeforme*)	The adult worms, ranging from 6 to 15 mms in length, attach themselves to the small intestines.	Anaemia, melena, weight loss, poor haircoat.	Larva penetrating the cat's skin, usually attacks the small intestine. Found in soil and flower gardens where faecal matter is deposited.	Fortnightly treatment with anthelmintics. Good sanitation (e.g. daily cleanup of litter boxes).
Tapeworm (*Dipylidium caninum* and *Taenia taeniformis*)	Up to 3 feet long. Parts shaped similar to cucumber seeds. The most common intermediate hosts are fleas and biting lice.	No clinical signs—difficult to detect.	Eating infected adult fleas. Uses rodents as hosts.	Praziquantel and epsiprantel. Management of environment to ensure scrupulously clean conditions. Proper flea control.

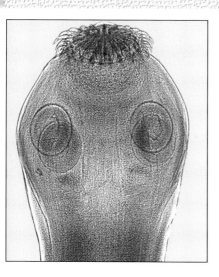

easy to control. If they are not controlled, they weaken the host cat to the point that other medical problems occur, but they are not dumb parasites.

HOOKWORMS

The worm *Ancylostoma tubaeforme* can inject a cat by larva penetrating its skin. It attaches itself to the small intestine of the cat, where it sucks blood. This loss of blood could cause iron-deficiency anaemia.

Outdoor cats that spend much of their time in the garden or in contact with soil are commonly injected with hookworm. There is another worm, the *Gordius* or horsehair worm, that, if ingested by a cat, causes vomiting.

TAPEWORMS

There are many species of tapeworms. They are carried by

DEWORMING

Ridding your kitten of worms is VERY IMPORTANT because certain worms that kittens carry, such as tapeworms and roundworms, can infect humans.

Breeders initiate a deworming programme at or about four weeks of age. The routine is repeated every two or three weeks until the kitten is three months old. The breeder from whom you obtained your kitten should provide you with the complete details of the deworming programme.

Your veterinary surgeon can prescribe and monitor the programme of deworming for you. The usual programme is treating the kitten every 15–20 days until the kitten is positively worm-free.

It is advised that you only treat your kitten with drugs that are recommended professionally.

The head and rostellum (the round prominence on the scolex) of a tapeworm, which infects cats and humans.

fleas! The cat eats the flea and starts the tapeworm cycle. Humans can also be infected with tapeworms, so don't eat fleas! Fleas are so small that your cat could pass them onto your hands, your plate or your food and thus make it possible for you to ingest a flea that is carrying tapeworm eggs.

While tapeworm infection is not life-threatening in cats (smart parasite!), it can be the cause of a

Magnified
heartworm
larvae,
*Dirofilaria
immitis.*

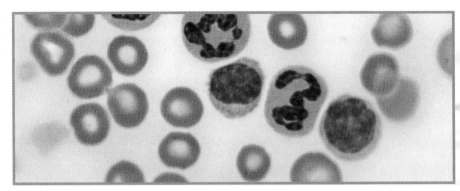

The
heartworm,
*Dirofilaria
immitis.*

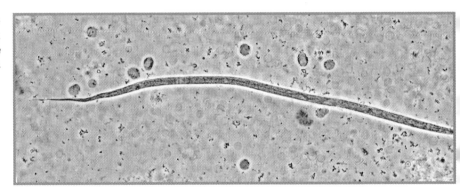

very serious liver disease for humans. About 50 percent of the humans infected with *Echinococcus multilocularis*, a type of tapeworm that causes alveolar hydatis, perish.

HEARTWORMS

Heartworms are thin, extended worms up to 30 cms (12 ins) long, which are difficult to diagnose in cats as the worms are too few to be identified by the antigen-detection test. Symptoms may be loss of energy, loss of appetite, coughing, the development of a pot belly and anaemia. Heartworm infection in cats should be treated very seriously as it is often fatal.

Heartworms are transmitted by mosquitoes. The mosquito drinks the blood of an infected cat and takes in larvae with the blood. It takes two to three weeks for the larvae to develop to the infective stage within the body of the mosquito. Cats are less frequently infected with heartworms than dogs are. Also, the parasite is more likely to attack the cat's brain or other organs rather than the heart. Cats should be treated at about six weeks of age, and maintained on a prophylactic dose given monthly.

THE FELINE EYE

by Lorraine Waters BvetNed, CertVOphthal, MRCVS

This part of the book aims to provide an owner's guide to feline ophthalmology. Ophthalmology is the study of eyes.

Eye diseases in the cat usually result from trauma, infection or neoplasia. Unlike the dog, the cat has few inherited eye conditions. Most of the conditions to be discussed are not amenable to first-aid measures or home remedies. Therefore, if you are at all worried about your cat's eyes, you should seek prompt veterinary attention.

Ocular pain is frequently associated with eye disease and can be recognised in your cat because it will show a combination of the following signs: blinking, increased tear production, fear of light and rubbing at the eye. Some conditions result in loss of vision; a gradual loss of vision may go unnoticed, as the cat slowly adapts, but a sudden loss produces an obvious change in behaviour. Being blind may not be as bad as it sounds, as cats adapt and cope amazingly well in familiar surroundings.

To examine the eye properly, veterinary surgeons first use a bright light, which allows close examination of the lids, conjunctiva, cornea and iris. Following this, an ophthalmoscope can be used, in a darkened room, to give a magnified view. Then by using the lenses within the ophthalmoscope, it is possible to focus on the structures further back in the eye, such as the lens, vitreous and retina.

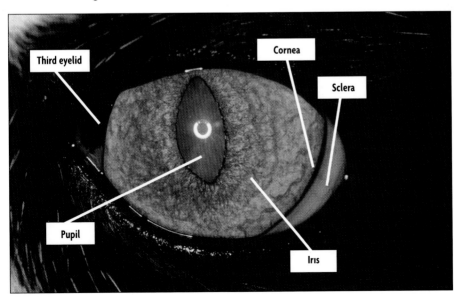

Third eyelid
Cornea
Sclera
Pupil
Iris

The feline
fundus, the eye
as seen through
the veterinary
surgeon's
ophthalmoscope.

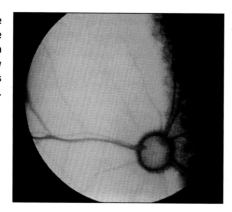

Topical ointments and drops are often prescribed for the treatment of eye disease. There are a few simple rules to follow when administering them. It is important to clean away discharges before applying treatment. Only give one drop or just a few millimetres of ointment; if you give too much, it will be diluted by increased tear production. Systemic drugs are those given by mouth to achieve higher concentrations at the back of the eye or for diseases which involve other body systems.

DISEASES OF THE FELINE EYE

GLOBE AND ORBIT
The eye sits in a bony socket in the skull known as the orbit. In short-nosed breeds, the orbit is shallow and the normal-sized eyes bulge forward. This situation can predispose the eye to a number of problems, such as exposure keratitis, overflow of tears and even prolapse of the globe (eye). Cats can be born with eyes that are too small and sink back into the orbit, to be covered by the third eyelid. This is non-inherited and usually associated with damage to the eye in utero. Abnormal enlargement of the globe may be congenital (buphthalmos) or acquired (hydrophthalmos) and is the end point of glaucoma.

The globe can prolapse from the orbit following head trauma, a common injury for cats involved in road traffic accidents. A minor prolapse replaced early can result in restoration of normal function. However, there is often stretching of the optic nerve and tearing of the extra-ocular muscles. In these cases the eye may be permanently damaged and have to be surgically removed. As an emergency measure, applying a moist cloth to the prolapsed eye on the way to the surgery will help preserve it.

Problems behind the eye become evident when they cause the eye to bulge forward along with the third eyelid. These include tooth root abscesses, foreign bodies, tumours and occasionally haemorrhage.

EYELIDS
The eyes of a kitten should open around 10–14 days of age. Once this has occurred, it is possible to see if the lids have been properly formed. Failure of all or part of the eyelids to develop is a rare congenital problem, known as coloboma. The

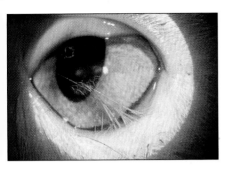

unprotected cornea, in the affected area, may become damaged and the lid must be surgically restored. Early infection in the eye may delay or prevent eyelid opening; the lids can be opened surgically to allow bathing and appropriate medication to be given.

Entropion and ectropion are common conditions in the dog and are related to conformation. Fortunately these are rare in cats and can be surgically corrected. Entropion secondary to ocular pain may remain once the cause of the pain is removed. Fortunately, these cases will respond to corrective surgery. Extra or abnormally positioned hairs are frequently seen as an inherited problem in dogs, but are rare in cats.

There are several types of tumours that can occur on the eyelids. The most common type is squamous cell carcinoma, more prevalent in white and part-white cats, as ultra-violet light (sunlight) plays a role in causing this condition. Treatment may consist of cryotherapy, surgical excision or radiation treatment. Early

recognition and treatment is essential to prevent destructive local spreading.

CONJUNCTIVA

The pink tissue lining the eyelid and covering the third eyelid and front of the sclera is called the conjunctiva. Dermoids are elements of skin tissue that arise in abnormal places. Dermoids often, but not invariably, contain hairs and can form on the conjunctiva and/or cornea. Dermoids act as foreign bodies in the eye, causing irritation and pain, and need to be surgically removed.

The most frequently encountered problem with the conjunctiva is conjunctivitis. In cats the majority of cases are infectious. An eye with conjunctivitis usually looks red and swollen with signs of ocular pain. Discharges may be watery or sticky yellow, indicating bacterial infection.

The most common infectious cause of feline conjunctivitis is feline herpesvirus (FHV). Feline calicivirus (FCV) can also cause conjunctivitis and is usually

Eyelid coloboma is a rare congenital problem in cats.

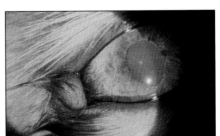

Dermoid in a longhaired cat.

Conjunctivitis, frequently an infectious disease in cats.

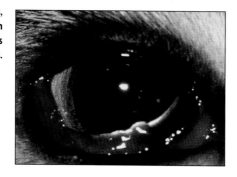

associated with other signs, such as upper respiratory tract signs and mouth ulcers. The bacteria *Chlamydia psittaci* can cause conjunctivitis in individual cats and in multi-cat households. Individual cases respond well to appropriate antibiotic therapy. Chronic and recurrent conjunctivitis in multi-cat situations requires thorough and prolonged treatment, management changes and, where appropriate, vaccination. *Mycoplasma spp.* can cause a less severe conjunctivitis than *Chlamydia spp.* Opportunistic infection can occur following cat-fight wounds, as bacteria are found on cats' teeth and claws.

Corneal ulcer stained with fluorescein.

Non-infectious causes of conjunctivitis include trauma,

foreign bodies, allergic disease, tumours and pre-corneal tear film abnormalities. Eosinophilic keratoconjunctivitis is a disease where the conjunctiva and cornea are invaded by cells from the immune system, primarily mast cells and eosinophils. These cells are responsible for inflammation and allergic reactions. This tends to occur in young to middle-aged cats and may be seasonal. Treatment usually works well but may be required long-term.

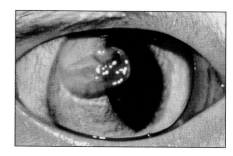

Several forms of neoplasia (cancer) can affect the conjunctiva in cats and can be either primary tumours arising in the conjunctiva or secondary, spreading from elsewhere in the body.

SCLERA

The sclera is the white fibrous coat of the globe. It is partially covered by the conjunctiva and protects the more fragile internal structures. Congenital defects of this structure are very rare. Inflammation (scleritis and episcleritis) is a problem in dogs and humans but extremely rare in cats. Feline

Tear staining is more commonly seen in short-nosed cat breeds.

scleral diseases are usually associated with trauma and neoplasia.

PRE-CORNEAL TEAR FILM

This forms from tears and moistens, lubricates and helps protect the cornea. Decreased tear production occurs if the tear glands are not working properly and results in a condition called 'dry eye' or keratoconjunctivis sicca (KCS). The cornea becomes dry and roughened, leading to keratitis and ulceration. It can occur following FHV infection, trauma, facial paralysis and chronic inflammation.

Overproduction of tears can be seen as a result of ocular pain. The naso-lacrimal duct drains the tears; it runs from the inner corner of the eye to just inside the end of the nose. Congenital defects, such as a small duct opening, result in tear overflow and staining around the eye. These can usually be corrected surgically. Acquired blockages may result from chronic conjunctivitis or foreign bodies.

Tear staining is also seen in short-nosed breeds because the

duct is tortuous and drainage inadequate. This is also associated with medial lower lid entropion, occluding the duct opening. This anatomical combination is very difficult to improve surgically.

Corneal foreign body.

CORNEA

The cornea is the clear circular area at the front of the eye through which the iris and pupil can be seen. Light passes through and is focused by the cornea, before passing through the lens and hence onto the retina. Congenital defects are rare but include micro- and megalocornea. There is sometimes a transient cloudiness following opening of the eyes but it should disappear by four weeks of age.

One of the most common problems involving the cornea is ulceration, where the top layer of corneal cells (the epithelium) is lost and the nerve endings exposed, resulting in ocular pain. Fluorescein is a special stain that can be used to demonstrate ulcers; they show up as a yellow/green patch on the cornea. If your cat has

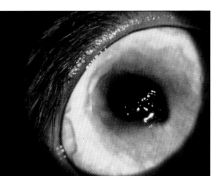

Corneal sequestrum.

Symblepharon, adhesion of the eyelid to the eyeball.

had this performed, you may have noticed the stain appearing at the end of its nose; this is because it drains down the naso-lacrimal duct and demonstrates that it is not blocked.

The most common cause of ulceration is trauma, from fight wounds or foreign bodies. FHV can cause ulceration. There is also a form of ulceration where the epithelium does not stick down again after healing and can easily become detached. This is seen as a breed-related problem in dogs. In cats it can be seen in older animals or associated with FHV infection, resulting in recurrent ulcer formation.

The cornea is very quick to repair ulcers, and, provided that the initial cause is removed, healing should only take a few days. Antibiotics are often applied to the eye while ulcers heal to prevent bacterial infection. Ulcers need prompt veterinary attention as they can deteriorate rapidly; deep ulcers can lead to rupture of

the eye and require urgent surgical repair.

The cornea is a common site for cat-scratch injuries and some may even penetrate the full thickness into the anterior chamber. If these wounds are repaired quickly and appropriate medical therapy is used, vision can usually be preserved. More severe ones may require reconstructive surgery, removal of the lens or even surgical removal of the eye.

Corneal foreign bodies usually result in ocular pain and need to be removed. Non-painful ones also need to be removed as they may penetrate the eye, causing internal problems.

Corneal sequestrum or necrosis is a condition specific to cats. The corneal stroma (middle layer) degenerates, turns brown/black and emerges through the epithelium, causing ulceration and a foreign body reaction with signs of ocular pain. These lesions usually need to be removed surgically because of the discomfort they cause, but a few will slough off naturally. Often a sequestrum will recur in the same eye or occur in the opposite eye at a later date. This condition is most commonly seen in Colourpoint Persians and is thought to have an inherited component. It may be related to their prominent eye position. The next most common breed with sequestra is the Burmese.

Following healing of a corneal

wound, there is usually formation of a scar, which shows up as a white mark, but unless they are extensive they do not usually affect vision.

TREATMENT AND MANAGEMENT OF FHV-RELATED EYE DISEASES

A combination of treatments is often required to treat feline herpesvirus (FHV) infection. In acute cases kittens are often very sick and need supportive treatment and intensive nursing. Systemic and topical antibiotics are used, sometimes in combination with topical antiviral drugs. Cats that develop symblepharon after acute infection may be blinded by the condition and require new reconstructive surgical techniques. The chronic cases can be difficult to diagnose and challenging to treat. Topical antivirals can be used and in non-ulcerated cases combined with corticosteroids. More recent treatments include L-lysine (to inhibit viral replication), Cimetidine and α-interferon (to boost the local immune response).

The reason for chronic FHV disease is that individuals become carriers of the virus. When they are stressed, the virus is reactivated and signs of infection and the cat's immune response to it manifest in the eye. This can be a major problem in multi-cat households, with carrier animals infecting kittens and adults alike. In these cases, management changes, including the identification of carriers, use of early vaccinations and isolation of new arrivals, must be instituted.

AQUEOUS HUMOUR

The aqueous humour is a watery fluid that is responsible for maintaining pressure within the eye. If the drainage angle is blocked and aqueous cannot drain away, pressure within the eye builds up, causing glaucoma. Glaucoma due to a congenitally obstructed drainage system is an inherited problem in many breeds of dog but is rare in the cat. When glaucoma does occur in cats, it is usually acquired, with drainage blocked by inflammatory or neoplastic cells.

Anterior uveitis can result in white blood cells in the anterior chamber, which gives it a cloudy look known as aqueous flare. Infection following penetrating wounds can result in pus accumulating in the chamber, known as hypopyon. Trauma to the eye and intra-ocular tumours may lead to bleeding into the anterior chamber (space behind the cornea

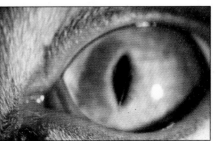

Herpesvirus ulcer.

Iris pigment change in an old cat.

and in front of the iris), known as hyphaema. This blood usually forms a clot and is absorbed. Foreign bodies can also occasionally be seen in the anterior chamber.

IRIS AND CILIARY BODY

The iris and ciliary body are muscular and vascular structures, which lie behind the cornea and in front of the lens. The iris is pigmented and gives the cat's eye its colour. Congenital defects are rare but occasionally cats are born with pieces of the iris missing. Changes in iris colour can occur for a number of reasons; as young cats mature, their iris colour may deepen. Inflammation results in reddening of the iris, due to an increase in blood vessel formation and engorgement, and is known as rubeosis iridis. Following inflammation, the iris can remain permanently dark.

As cats age, they can develop a condition called melanosis. This is usually, but not always, a diffuse

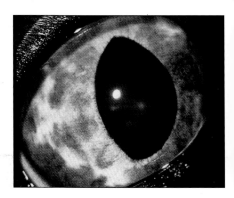

change, occurring slowly in both eyes. It must be monitored and differentiated from iris melanoma. Melanoma is a tumour of the pigment cells that can result in either diffuse or nodular discoloration of the iris. It usually progresses quickly and only in one eye. This type of neoplasia has a potential to spread outside the eye and is usually treated by surgically removing the affected eye.

A difference in colour between the two irises is known as heterochromia iridis and can occur naturally in white or poorly pigmented breeds, usually associated with congenital deafness. In other cats, it usually indicates a problem in one eye or the other.

The ciliary body and iris are known as the anterior uvea, while the choroid (the vascular layer that lies between the retina and the sclera and provides a blood supply to the retina) is the posterior uvea. Uveitis is an inflammation of the uvea. It may involve both the

Iris melanoma, exhibited as a tumour of pigment cells that results in discoloration of the iris.

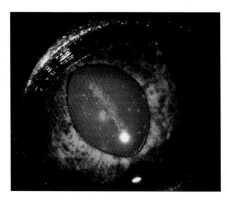

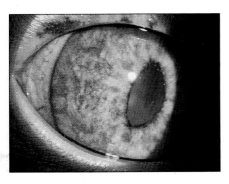

Uveitis, inflammation of the iris, ciliary body and choroid.

anterior and posterior uvea and has many causes in the cat. The main infectious causes are feline immunodeficiency virus (FIV), feline leukaemia virus (FeLV), feline infectious peritonitis (FIP) and toxoplasmosis. Tuberculosis has been reported in cats as a cause of uveitis and, in sub-tropical and tropical countries, fungal infection can be a significant cause. The signs of uveitis for all these diseases are very similar and may include a constricted pupil, rubeosis iridis, aqueous flare, poor vision and ocular pain. It can be difficult to determine the cause in some cases despite thorough investigation. Even if the primary viral infection cannot be cured, cats with uveitis can be treated symptomatically to ease discomfort and maintain vision. Long-term uveitis can lead to cataract formation, lens luxation and glaucoma. Non-infectious causes of uveitis include trauma and neoplasia.

Atrophy of the iris may occur as a result of ageing or following inflammation. Cysts of the iris are sometimes seen and look like black balloons. They form on the back of the iris but can detach and float through the pupil to rest in front. They are not neoplastic and do not usually need to be removed.

LENS

The lens is the clear disc-shaped structure suspended behind the iris, responsible for focusing light onto the retina. A cataract, or opacity of the lens and/or its capsule, is a disorder of the lens. Many forms of hereditary cataract are seen in dogs but not in cats. Congenital cataracts are occasionally found as a non-inherited problem. Most of the cataracts seen in cats are formed secondary to lens damage, e.g. blunt trauma, penetrating wounds, chronic anterior uveitis and lens luxation. If cataracts involve the whole lens, light will not be able to get through to the retina and the eye will be rendered blind. If appropriate, cataracts can be surgically removed.

If the lens's suspensory fibres weaken or break, it will become dislocated and can fall into either the back or front of the eye. This is

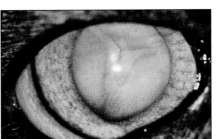

Cataract developed from long-term uveitis.

a common breed-related problem in terrier dogs and is occasionally seen in cats, usually as a result of trauma, ageing or cataract. The lens is usually surgically removed to prevent it from blocking the pupil, which can lead to glaucoma.

The lens condenses with age, giving it a grey appearance, known as senile sclerosis. This is not a true cataract as light can still pass through to the back of the eye and vision is not impaired.

One rare but important condition of the lens in the cat is post-traumatic sarcoma. If the lens is damaged by trauma, it can become neoplastic and rapidly fill the eye with tumours. Appropriate treatment at the time of the initial injury should prevent this, but when it does occur, surgical removal of the eye is recommended.

VITREOUS HUMOUR

The vitreous humour is a jelly-like substance that fills the space between the back of the lens and the front of the retina. Like the aqueous humour, the vitreous can be infiltrated with haemorrhage and inflammatory cells. Foreign bodies can occasionally be found in the vitreous. Inflammation of the vitreous, known as hyalitis, can be seen as part of generalised uveitis.

Vitreous degenerates with age, giving a cloudy appearance to the back of the eye, but this does not usually affect vision to any great extent.

THINGS TO LOOK OUT FOR

A change in appearance of the eye
- Redness
- Cloudiness
- Change in iris colour

Increase in discharges
- Watery

Sticky mucoid
- Yellow
- Bloody

Blinking, squinting and head shyness
Aversion to light
Rubbing at the eye
Loss of vision
Protrusion of the eye
Loss of facial symmetry

RETINA

The retina, at the back of the eye, is where the visual image is formed. Congenital retinal problems are rare in cats, but colobomas (defects or holes) can occasionally be seen in the optic disc (the point at which nerves converge to leave the eye as the optic nerve).

Inflammation of the retina usually occurs together with inflammation of the choroid and is called chorioretinitis or posterior uveitis. The causes are the same as those for anterior uveitis. Inflammation can lead to retinal detachment, haemorrhage, degeneration and scarring of the retina. It can be difficult to diagnose the cause of posterior uveitis; symptomatic treatment is generally given to maintain vision.

The retina may also degenerate

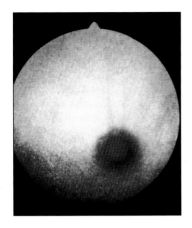

as a result of non-inflammatory processes. An inherited form of retinal degeneration has been described in the Abyssinian and Siamese breeds. Deficiency in dietary taurine (an amino acid) causes retinal degeneration. Fortunately, this is now rare as proprietary cat foods are supplemented with this compound. It may, however, still be a problem with some home prepared diets.

Hypertension is a common cause of retinal disease in elderly cats. It may be primary, essential hypertension or secondary to other diseases, such as kidney disease, hyperthyroidism and diabetes. Hypertension causes changes in the retinal arteries, retinal and vitreal haemorrhages, retinal detachment and hyphaema. Early recognition and treatment are essential to prevent permanent ocular damage and damage to other organs, such as the kidney, heart and brain.

Retinal detachment causes blindness and may result from hypertension, inflammation and neoplasia. If the retina does not reattach in 24–48 hours, there will be permanent vision loss. Symptomatic treatment is often given to reattach the retina, but it is also important to treat the underlying cause.

Retinal haemorrhages can occur as a result of hypertension, inflammation and trauma. They can cause temporary loss of vision but will often be resorbed. Once again it is important to find the underlying cause and treat it accordingly without delay.

Finally, if in any doubt regarding the condition of your cat's eyes, it is always worthwhile consulting your veterinary surgeon. Even if you consider the condition minor, it may not remain so!

Advanced retinal degeneration.

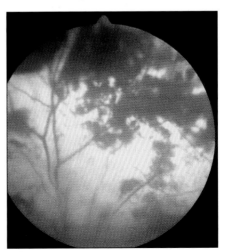

Retinal haemorrhages as a result of hypertension.

The author is grateful to the Animal Health Trust (England) for the illustrations used in the eye health section.

INDEX

C3117

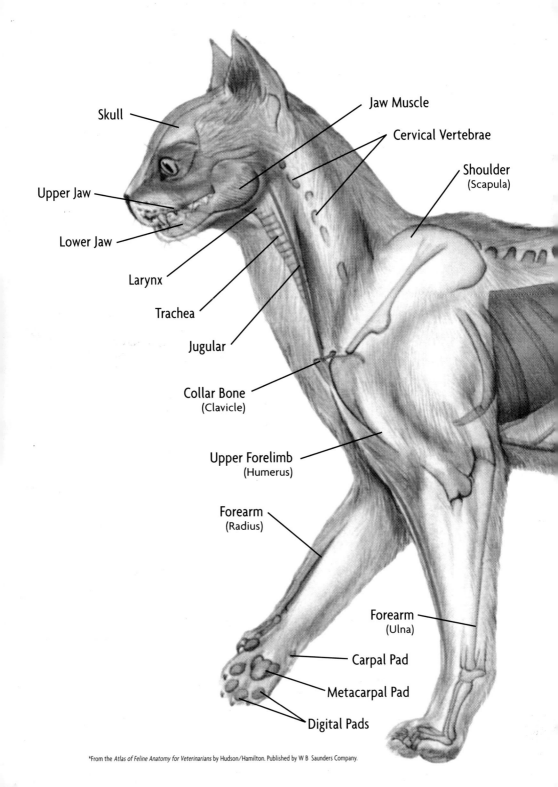

Skull

Jaw Muscle

Cervical Vertebrae

Upper Jaw

Shoulder
(Scapula)

Lower Jaw

Larynx

Trachea

Jugular

Collar Bone
(Clavicle)

Upper Forelimb
(Humerus)

Forearm
(Radius)

Forearm
(Ulna)

Carpal Pad

Metacarpal Pad

Digital Pads

*From the *Atlas of Feline Anatomy for Veterinarians* by Hudson/Hamilton. Published by W B Saunders Company.